# MYTHOLOGY

*Edith Hamilton*

SPARK PUBLISHING

© 2003, 2007 by Spark Publishing, A Division of Barnes & Noble

This Spark Publishing edition 2014 by SparkNotes LLC, an Affiliate of Barnes & Noble

All rights reserved. No part of this publication may be reproduced, stored in a retrieval system, or transmitted in any form or by any means (including electronic, mechanical, photocopying, recording, or otherwise) without prior written permission from the publisher.

122 Fifth Avenue
New York, NY 10011
www.sparknotes.com

ISBN 978-1-4114-6952-5

Please submit changes or report errors to www.sparknotes.com/errors.

Printed in Canada

10 9 8 7 6 5

# Contents

| | |
|---|---|
| CONTEXT | 1 |
| OVERVIEW | 4 |
| CHARACTER LIST | 6 |
| ANALYSIS OF MAJOR CHARACTERS | 15 |
|     ZEUS | 15 |
|     ODYSSEUS | 15 |
|     OEDIPUS | 16 |
|     MEDEA | 17 |
| THEMES, MOTIFS & SYMBOLS | 18 |
|     THE DOMINANCE OF FATE | 18 |
|     BLOODSHED BEGETS BLOODSHED | 19 |
|     THE DANGER OF ARROGANCE AND HUBRIS | 20 |
|     REWARD FOR GOODNESS AND RETRIBUTION FOR EVIL | 20 |
|     THE HERO'S QUEST | 21 |
|     BEAUTY | 21 |
|     LOVE | 22 |
|     CANNIBALISM | 22 |
|     ART | 23 |
| SUMMARY & ANALYSIS | 24 |
|     INTRODUCTION TO CLASSICAL MYTHOLOGY | 24 |
|     PART ONE, CHAPTERS I–II | 27 |
|     PART ONE, CHAPTERS III–IV | 31 |
|     PART TWO, CHAPTERS I–II | 36 |
|     PART TWO, CHAPTERS III–IV | 40 |
|     PART THREE, CHAPTERS I–II | 44 |
|     PART THREE, CHAPTERS III–IV | 48 |
|     PART FOUR, CHAPTERS I–II | 52 |
|     PART FOUR, CHAPTER III — THE ADVENTURES OF ODYSSEUS | 56 |
|     PART FOUR, CHAPTER IV — THE ADVENTURES OF AENEAS | 60 |
|     PART FIVE, CHAPTERS I–II | 64 |
|     PART FIVE, CHAPTER III; PART SIX, CHAPTERS I–II | 69 |
|     PART SEVEN, INTRODUCTION & CHAPTERS I–II | 73 |

| IMPORTANT QUOTATIONS EXPLAINED | 77 |
| --- | --- |
| KEY FACTS | 81 |
| STUDY QUESTIONS | 83 |
| **HOW TO WRITE LITERARY ANALYSIS** | **85** |
| THE LITERARY ESSAY: A STEP-BY-STEP GUIDE | 85 |
| SUGGESTED ESSAY TOPICS | 97 |
| A+ STUDENT ESSAY | 98 |
| GLOSSARY OF LITERARY TERMS | 100 |
| A NOTE ON PLAGIARISM | 102 |
| REVIEW & RESOURCES | 103 |
| QUIZ | 103 |
| SUGGESTIONS FOR FURTHER READING | 108 |

# Context

ALTHOUGH HER NAME IS THE ONLY ONE on the cover, Edith Hamilton is not really the author of all the tales in *Mythology*. It is more accurate to think of her as a collector or interpreter, as she compiled the stories in the book from the writings of various Greek, Roman, and Icelandic authors. Nevertheless, Hamilton's choices reflect a personal point of view: the stories she includes, her methods of storytelling, and her omissions reveal her own interpretation of the myths and also reflect the time period in which she was writing.

Hamilton was born in 1867 to an American family living in Dresden, Germany, and grew up in Fort Wayne, Indiana. In 1894, she graduated from Bryn Mawr, a women's school in Baltimore, and was then appointed headmistress there in 1896. In 1922, she retired from her headmistress position to focus on her writing and her studies of ancient Greek and Roman civilization. Hamilton's experiences at Bryn Mawr undoubtedly affected the perspective of *Mythology*, where the theme of women struggling in a male-dominated world runs throughout the text. She died in 1963, having been made an honorary citizen of Athens, an award that signified what she considered the pinnacle of her life.

Hamilton wrote a number of well-known books about Greek and Roman life, most notably *The Greek Way* (1930) and *The Roman Way* (1932). These books, along with *Mythology*, became standard interpretations of classical life and art, as Hamilton focused on the ways Greek and Roman value systems serve as the foundation for modern European and American societies. She wrote the books between World Wars I and II, and they clearly reflect the search for cultural roots that many felt was needed during that historical period. Written in a time of great upheaval—the global economic Depression and Europe's disintegration before World War II—*Mythology*'s focus on the shared, broad, and ancient cultural heritage of America and Europe gave the book widespread appeal.

Again, Hamilton is not the original author of these myths, but their compiler from a variety of classical poets from ancient Greek and Roman civilization. Greek civilization flowered first, generating the paradigms, frameworks, and myths that the Romans later adopted. The earliest poet Hamilton uses is a Greek one—Homer, who is said to have composed the *Iliad* and the *Odyssey* around 1,000 B.C.. These two works are the two oldest known Greek texts and are—with their clear and widespread influence—considered fundamental texts of Western culture and literature. Their depictions of heroism have provided models for social morals and ethics that still resonate today. Their imaginative power has achieved no less: their characters, images, and narratives have continued to fascinate generations of readers and guide multitudes of artists.

Hamilton draws from a number of other authors besides Homer: other Greeks, such as Hesiod, Pindar, Aeschylus, Sophocles, and Euripides, and Romans such as Ovid, Virgil, and Apollodorus. At the beginning of each chapter, Hamilton notes which authors she has used as source material for that chapter's stories. Such citations are important, as these different authors—widely separated by time and worldview—tell radically different kinds of stories. Hamilton's introduction offers a chronological overview of these original authors, reminding us that the Romans wrote roughly 1,000 years after Homer and about 500 years after the Greek tragedians. This time difference is significant, as the warring, fractious conglomeration of independent Greek city-states made for a very different society from the immense, stately Roman Empire, the largest and most stable empire the world had ever seen. Augustus's Rome was a rich, sophisticated, and decadent culture, and its literature reflects this spirit. Whereas myths were very practical for the Greek authors, defining their religion and explaining the world around them, Roman authors treated the myths as elaborate fantasies told purely for entertainment or as cultural hallmarks that were used to justify Roman world dominance as a divinely decreed manifest destiny.

These contrasting motivations of the classical poets, and the degree to which such motivations are reflected in their stories, remind us that even these Greek and Roman poets were not themselves the original creators of these myths. Each written retelling of a myth was merely a new version of an old story that had been told countless times before in Greek and Roman oral and written tradition. Yet each new telling represents a new interpretation that shifts emphases and draws connections not previously made. Therefore, whether intentionally or not, each retelling radiates a new and different meaning. The same may be said here of Hamilton and her retelling in *Mythology*.

## Brief Historical Context

The idea of "ancient Greece" itself is problematic: for most of its history, the country was disunified, comprising frequently warring city-states, each with its own culture and history. Myths largely emerged from Athens, the most dominant of the city-states and the one that especially encouraged intellectual and artistic pursuits. It is not surprising, then, that the greatest literary legacy of ancient Greece would emerge from this dominant city.

The greatest Greek epics, the *Iliad* and *Odyssey* of Homer, were written during the Greek Middle Ages (roughly 1100–700 B.C.), most likely around 1000 B.C. These epics evolved from a long oral tradition that Homer supposedly transcribed, but his single authorship is disputed. Greek society transformed from its Dark Ages to the city-state society that would dominate the next several centuries. Over the course of this time, overseas trade prospered, with Athens and Sparta its principal cities. The Persian War (490–479 B.C.) gave Athens its first great glory, proving itself a naval power. Athenian culture blossomed, as the great tragic poets Aeschylus, Sophocles, and Euripides competed in the renowned Athenian drama festivals. Myth, literature, and drama flourished. This Athenian golden age is generally regarded as the period 478–431 B.C., ending the year Athens became embroiled in the Peloponnesian War with Sparta. Athens lost the war and their dominance in the region in 404 B.C.

In 358 B.C., King Philip of Macedonia began a conquest that eventually brought all of Greece under his rule. After his murder in 336 B.C., his son Alexander the Great inherited and expanded the empire until his death in 323 B.C. During the Hellenistic Period (323–146 B.C.), Alexander's empire was divided, and Alexandria, Egypt, became the new cultural and literary center of the region.

Around 200 B.C., the emergent civilization in Rome began a process of overseas conquest and expansion. By the 140s B.C., the entire Greek empire had become a Roman province. The Romans, enamored with Greek culture and art, adopted much of it. After Caesar's murder in 44 B.C., a period of turmoil enveloped the Empire. Octavian, Caesar's grand-nephew, assumed control after his great defeat of Marc Anthony at Actium in 31 B.C. He later became known as Augustus, whose reign from 31 B.C.–A.D. 14 was a time of great prosperity and expansion for Rome. Virgil and Ovid, the most famous Roman literary figures, wrote during this period.

# Overview

**M**YTHOLOGY resembles one large SparkNote in itself, offering a detailed overview of the myths of ancient Greece and Rome and a brief overview of Norse mythology. Since a tradition as immense as classical mythology cannot be presented in any linear fashion, *Mythology* frequently contains references to characters or stories that are not explained until later. Nonetheless, it is perfectly acceptable to skip around in the book to alleviate this confusion whenever it arises.

Hamilton begins by providing her rationale for the study of mythology and her understanding of its nature. She then introduces the major gods and describes the creation of the universe. Twelve primary gods live together on Mount Olympus: Zeus, the chief of these Olympians, is joined by his wife (and sister) Hera; his daughter Athena; his sons Hermes and Ares; the brother-and-sister pair Apollo and Artemis (also Zeus's children); Zeus's brothers Poseidon and Hades; his sister Hestia; and Hephaestus and his wife Aphrodite (both sometimes considered to be Zeus's children as well). The names of these gods are Greek in origin, but the Romans renamed most of the gods when they adopted them. Except in cases when a story is told exclusively by a Roman author, Hamilton employs the original Greek names in her retelling. Besides these twelve are two other important gods—Zeus's sister Demeter and his son Dionysus—who live on earth rather than on Mount Olympus.

According to classical mythology, the universe began in a manner that—remarkably—resembles the modern scientific theory of the big bang. There was originally only chaos and darkness. Out of the swirling energy Earth and Heaven arose and gave birth to many children. Though most of these children were monsters, they eventually gave rise to the Titans, a race of gods in human form. One of the Titans overthrew his sky-father, only to see his own son Zeus overthrow him later.

Zeus and his siblings defeated all the Titans in a fierce battle and installed themselves as the lords of the universe. They created humankind and promptly began manipulating their new creatures. Zeus, an incurable philanderer, frequently descended to Earth, often in some magical form, to have his way with beautiful human women. The offspring of these liaisons grew to be the first heroes among humankind and, with the gods' aid, won many victories against vicious monsters and completed monumental tasks. Many of these half-divine heroes, along with their few all-mortal peers, went on to found the dynasties of Greece. The most notable of these heroes are Theseus, Hercules, Cadmus, Achilles, and Aeneas.

The stories about these heroes, which account for the founding of certain cities or the legitimacy of certain dynastic bloodlines, were meant to explain phenomena that the Greeks observed in the world around them. The Greeks also told many other tales, often of a nonheroic nature, to explain the qualities of flowers, lightning, landscapes, and so on. Indeed, as Hamilton writes, these myths can be seen as "early science." Much of classical myth, however, is far more complex than these simple explanatory tales. The works of the Greek playwrights, written around 500 B.C., portray a rich, complex social and ethical fabric and are sensitive to the most profound issues of the human condition. The protagonists of these plays, caught in webs of circumstances beyond their control, have to nonetheless face their situations and make moral decisions of direst consequence to themselves and others. Many scholars consider these Greek tragedies to be as sophisticated in their psychology and writing as anything penned since.

Hamilton reserves a final section for the traditions of the Norsemen. Unlike the Greek and Roman stories, which have been retold in many versions that still exist today, the Norse tales have barely survived. Christian obsession with the destruction of pagan material swept clean Scandinavia, Germany, and other Norse areas. Only in Iceland did written versions of Norse tales survive. These Icelandic texts, which date from about 1300 A.D. but reflect a much older oral tradition, depict a bleak, dismal, and ultimately doomed universe, headed for a day of battle between good and evil in which even the gods will be destroyed. Though Hamilton's treatment of Norse myth is brief, it does offer a striking contrast to the comparatively sunny world of Mediterranean myth.

# Character List

## The Olympians

*Zeus*  Roman name: Jupiter or Jove. The sky-god Zeus rules Mount Olympus. His weapon is the thunderbolt, and his bird is the eagle. The central figure of the myths, Zeus epitomizes their complexity. At times he is divine and represents a pure, eternal sense of justice; at other times, he is capricious and cruel.

*Hera*  Roman name: Juno. Zeus's wife and sister, Hera is a very powerful goddess known mostly for her jealousy. She is often vicious and spiteful, and it is usually Zeus's infidelity that incites her. Many unfortunate mortals endure hardships by provoking Hera's wrath.

*Poseidon*  Roman name: Neptune. The god of the sea, Poseidon is Zeus's brother and second only to him in power. Poseidon holds a decade-long grudge against Odysseus. The often cruel and unpredictable violence of the seas is assumed to be a result of his anger.

*Hades*  Roman name: Pluto. The brother of Zeus and Poseidon, Hades rules the underworld, the realm of the dead, with his wife, Persephone.

*Pallas Athena*  Roman name: Minerva. Usually just called Athena, this goddess emerges from Zeus's head fully-grown and armed. Associated with war, cleverness, and wit, it is no surprise that she favors Odysseus. Athena is the goddess of Wisdom, Reason, and Purity and is chaste, like Artemis and Hestia.

*Phoebus Apollo*  Usually just called Apollo. A son of Zeus and Leto and Artemis's twin, he is the god of Light and Truth, the master of Poetry and Music, and the god of Archery. His Oracle at Delphi is revered for her powers of prophecy and truth.

*Artemis*  Roman name: Diana. Apollo's twin sister, Artemis is the beautiful huntress goddess and, like Athena, is somewhat masculine. Artemis is normally good and just, but demands a human sacrifice during the Trojan War.

*Aphrodite*  Roman name: Venus. Aphrodite is the sweet and delicate goddess of Love, Beauty, and Romance. Even so, she often shows formidable power, as in the story of Cupid and Psyche, and is herself a principal cause of the Trojan War. In a strange twist, lovely Aphrodite is married to the ugly and crippled Hephaestus.

*Hermes*  Roman name: Mercury. Hermes is the son of Zeus and the Titan Atlas's daughter Maia. The messenger of the gods, he is fast and cunning. Hermes is a master thief, the god of Commerce and the Market, and the guide who leads the dead from Earth to Hades.

*Ares*  Roman name: Mars. A vicious god, Ares is hated by both his father, Zeus, and mother, Hera. The god of War, he is always bloody and ruthless, yet we see in his vain bullying that he is also, paradoxically, a coward.

*Hephaestus*  Roman name: Vulcan or Mulciber. Hephaestus is either the son of Zeus and Hera, or simply of Hera alone, who gives birth to him in retaliation for Zeus's solo fathering of Athena. The only ugly Olympian, he is also partially crippled. Hephaestus is the armorer and smith of the gods, and he forges spectacular magical objects. He is kind, generous, and good-natured.

## OTHER GODS, DEITIES & SUPERNATURAL BEINGS

*Earth*  Also known as Gaea or Mother Earth. She is the first being to emerge in the universe, born somehow out of the forces of Love, Light, and Day. She gives birth to Heaven, who then becomes her husband. This story is vastly different from the Christian creation myth, in which a deity exists first and then fashions the Earth.

*Heaven*    Also known as Ouranos or Father Heaven. Born out of Earth, he becomes Earth's husband and proceeds to father all the original creatures of the earth, including the Titans, the Cyclopes, and the Furies.

*The Titans*    The original gods, children of Heaven and Earth, and parents of the six original Olympians. Defeated by Zeus and his siblings in a war for control of the universe, most of the Titans are imprisoned in the bowels of the earth. Prometheus, who sides with Zeus, and his two brothers, Epimetheus and Atlas, are not imprisoned. Atlas is forced to carry the weight of the world on his shoulders forever.

*Cronus*    Roman name: Saturn. Cronus becomes the ruler of the Titans by overthrowing his father Ouranos. He swallows each of his children as his wife Rhea gives birth to them. Rhea is able to save one, Zeus, who forces Cronus to vomit up his siblings, with whom he defeats the Titans for control of the universe.

*Prometheus*    One of the most enduring figures in Greek myth, Prometheus is the only Titan to side with Zeus against Cronus. He repeatedly defies the gods by helping humans, most notably by bringing them fire from Olympus. Though Zeus devises a cruel torture for him, chaining him to a rock where every day an eagle comes to pick at his innards, Prometheus never surrenders.

*Dionysus*    Dionysus, or Bacchus, god of wine. He embodies both the good and evil effects of alcohol. At times he is a jovial partier and patron of music and art, but at other times he is the god of madness and frenzy.

*Demeter*    Roman name: Ceres. Though a sister of Zeus, Demeter lives on earth. Demeter is the goddess of corn and harvest. She is kinder than Dionysus but also sadder, mostly because Hades has taken her daughter, Persephone, as his reluctant bride. Demeter thus lies in mourning for four months of the year, leaving the fields barren.

*Persephone*  Roman name: Proserpine. The beautiful daughter of Demeter whom Hades kidnaps to be his wife. She is usually passive, agreeing to whatever is asked of her. Once she even places some of her beauty in a box.

*Eros*  Roman name: Cupid. The son of Aphrodite. Eros uses his bow to fire magic arrows that cause people to fall in love. He is a beautiful young man, though he is typically depicted as a winged cherub. Eros, who is often blindfolded, performs works of romantic mischief whenever Aphrodite asks.

*The Furies*  Also known as the Erinyes, the Furies are three horrible sisters—Tisiphone, Megaera, and Alecto—who torment evildoers and punish them for their sins.

*The Fates*  Three mysterious sisters who affect the paths of all in the universe. Clotho spins the thread of life, Lachesis assigns each person's thread, and Atropos snips the thread of life at its end. Since fate is the only force to rule above both gods and men, the fates arguably have more power than anyone else in the Greek universe.

## Famous Heroes & Heroines

*Odysseus*  Roman name: Ulysses. Odysseus is the protagonist of Homer's *Odyssey*. He is the king of Ithaca and a great warrior in the Trojan War but is best known for his decade-long trip home from the war. Odysseus survives the challenges he encounters by using his wits. A fine talker and brilliant strategist, he is perhaps the most modern and human of the classical heroes.

*Hercules*  Another famous Greek hero, a son of Zeus who rises to Olympus at his death. Hercules is renowned for his incredible strength and bravery, but he lacks intelligence and self-control. Most of his adventures begin with a horrible mistake that he makes and then attempts to fix. His most famous feats, the Twelve Labors of Hercules, are the punishment he receives for murdering his family in a fit of madness.

*Theseus* — The son of King Aegeus of Athens and a quintessential Athenian hero. Theseus is the model citizen: a kind leader, good to his friends and countrymen. Theseus does have his shortcomings, however: he abandons Ariadne, and later doubts his own son, which leads to his tragic demise.

*Jason* — One of the least impressive of the Greek heroes. Jason's most notable feat is his assembly of a cast of heroes to travel on a long fraudulent quest—the recovery of the Golden Fleece. When Jason arrives in Colchis to retrieve the Fleece, the daughter of the king, Medea, falls in love with him. Jason abandons her and marries a princess later for political gain. In revenge, Medea kills Jason's new wife and her own children, whom Medea had by Jason. Though he lives on, he bears the burden of this tragedy, in some ways a fate worse than death.

*Perseus* — Zeus's son by the beautiful princess Danaë. Danaë's father, forewarned that Perseus will someday kill him, locks the infant and his mother in a trunk and casts it into the sea. Perseus survives, comes of age, and sets out to kill the monster Medusa and bring back her head. As prophesied, he kills his grandfather, though unwittingly, by hitting him with a stray discus.

*Oedipus* — The son of the king of Thebes. Oedipus frees Thebes from the menace of the Sphinx and marries the widowed queen, Jocasta, unaware that she is his mother. Learning the truth later, he faces fate and blinds himself as penance.

*Orestes* — The hero of the *Oresteia*, Aeschylus's trilogy of plays. Orestes's father is the great king Agamemnon, leader of the Greeks in the Trojan War, and his sister is the sacrificed Iphigenia. When his mother, Clytemnestra, kills Agamemnon to avenge Iphigenia's death, Orestes kills her. As a result, the horrible Furies plague him until he atones for his crime.

## Characters of the Trojan War

*Paris*     A son of King Priam of Troy, Paris unwittingly starts the Trojan War by judging Aphrodite the fairest of all the goddesses. Aphrodite arranges for Paris to marry the beautiful Helen, but Helen is already married. Helen's kidnapping leads the Greeks to unite against Troy and sparks the decade-long Trojan War. Paris is only a minor figure in the Trojan War battles and is usually portrayed as weak and unheroic.

*Helen*     The most beautiful woman who has ever lived, Helen is promised to Paris after his judgment of Aphrodite. Her kidnapping causes the Trojan War. Helen is peculiarly silent in the *Iliad,* living with Paris for ten years before returning home with Menelaus, her original husband. Helen is treated as more of an object than a person.

*Hector*     Another son of King Priam, Hector is the bravest and most famous of the Trojan warriors. Unlike his brother Paris, he faces challenges with great strength and courage. His death ends the *Iliad*.

*Aeneas*     The only great Trojan warrior who survives the war, Aeneas is protected by Aphrodite, his mother. He flees Troy, carrying his father on his back and leading his child by the hand. His values are more Roman than Greek, as he is first and foremost a warrior.

*Agamemnon*     One the great kings who leads the Greeks in the Trojan War and whose story continues in the *Oresteia*. Agamemnon's stubbornness toward Achilles almost costs the Greeks the war, and his cold-hearted sacrifice of his daughter Iphigenia ultimately costs him his life.

*Achilles*    The most famous Greek in the Trojan War, whose strength and bravery are unrivaled. Achilles is selfless, courageous, and devoted to the gods—he is the finest Greek warrior. His mother, the sea-nymph Thetis, has made him invulnerable everywhere except his heel, and that is where he is struck and killed.

## OTHER CHARACTERS

*Pandora*    The first and most famously foolish woman of Greek myth. Married to Epimetheus, Prometheus's simple-minded brother, she has been entrusted with a box that the gods have told her never to open. Pandora peeks inside the box, unleashing evil into the world. She manages to close the box just in time to save Hope, humankind's only solace.

*Orpheus*    A son of one of the Muses, Orpheus is the greatest mortal musician who has ever lived. His most famous exploit is his journey to Hades to retrieve his dead wife, Eurydice. He loses her forever by ignoring Hades' orders and turning to make sure she is behind him. Orpheus also travels on the *Argo* and protects Jason and the others from the Sirens. He is killed by a pack of roving Maenads, and his head floats to Lesbos, where it becomes a magical icon.

*Oracle at Delphi*    A priestess of Apollo and the most famous prophet in all of Greece. Humans typically consult the Oracle to ascertain the will of the gods or a person's fate. She most often appears at the beginning of a story, as a character asks his fate, finds it unpleasant, and then tries to change it—only to become a victim of fate precisely because of his efforts to change it.

*Ariadne*    The daughter of King Minos of Crete. Ariadne falls in love with the hero Theseus and uses a golden thread to help him defeat the Labyrinth of the dreaded Minotaur.

*Medea* — Along with Circe, Medea is one of two famous sorceresses in Greek myth. Medea selflessly helps Jason defeat her own father and obtain the Golden Fleece. After Jason turns on her, she kills his new wife and then her own children.

*Iphigenia* — The daughter whom Agamemnon offers at Aulis as the human sacrifice that Artemis demands. In one version of the myth, Artemis saves Iphigenia and makes her a priestess who conducts human sacrifices. In this version, Iphigenia is rescued by her brother, Orestes.

## Monsters

*Medusa* — One of the three Gorgons. Medusa is a horrible woman-beast with snakes for hair. Her gaze turns men to stone. She is killed by Perseus.

*The Minotaur* — The half-man, half-bull monster that terrorizes Minos's Labyrinth. It is killed by Theseus.

*The Sphinx* — A beast with the head of a woman and the body of a winged lion. The Sphinx blocks entry to the city of Thebes, refusing to budge until someone answers her riddle and eating anyone who fails. When Oedipus solves the riddle, the Sphinx promptly kills herself.

*The Cyclopes* — Fearsome one-eyed giants, of whom Polyphemus is the most famous. In some myths they are the children of Heaven and Earth; in others they are the sons of Poseidon. They forge the thunderbolts of Zeus, who favors them.

*Polyphemus* — The terrible Cyclops who imprisons Odysseus and his men and eats them alive. They escape only after blinding him. In later myths, he becomes a pitiful character who recovers his sight but chases after the cruel nymph Galatea who mocks him.

*Cerberus* — A vile three-headed dog that guards the gates of Hades.

# Norse Mythology

*Odin* — The counterpart of Zeus in Norse mythology. Odin is a quiet, brooding figure. He trades one of his eyes and suffers for nine nights to attain the insights of the Well of Wisdom, which he passes on to men along with the mystical powers of the runes and poetry. Odin rewards fallen warriors with a place in Valhalla, the Hall of the Slain. He bears the burden of delaying Ragnarok, the day of doom for both the gods and mortals, as long as possible.

*Hela* — A fearful goddess who presides over the realm of the dead, which is called Hel (not synonymous with our word "hell," however). The fact that a female occupies this position is a significant and striking difference from Greek and Roman myth.

*The Valkyries* — The "Choosers of the Slain," these splendid female warriors select and carry dead warriors to Valhalla.

*Signy* — Signy, wronged by her husband, conceives a son with her brother Sigmund. She bides her time until the son is old enough to help Sigmund kill her husband. Signy then kills herself by walking into the fire that also consumes her husband and her other children.

*Sigurd* — Sigmund's son, a fierce warrior who braves a ring of fire for the love of the beautiful woman-warrior Brynhild. Sigmund is always honest, brave, fierce, and giving, thus embodying the ideal Norse warrior. He is the prototype for Siegfried, popularized in Wagner's *Ring Cycle*.

*Brynhild* — A Valkyrie who angers Odin and is punished with imprisonment in a ring of fire. She is a dazzling character, with strength both of soul and body. She is the prototype for Wagner's Brunnhilde, the most famous Valkyrie in opera.

# Analysis of Major Characters

## Zeus

Though Zeus (Jupiter or Jove) is the closest figure in mythology to an omnipotent ruler, he is far from all-powerful. He also lacks the perfection we might expect in a divine ruler. However, this imperfection is only a detriment if we view Zeus as a moral authority, which, according to his stories, he is not. Hamilton portrays Zeus as both an agent and victim of fate. As ruler of the gods, Zeus is destined to overthrow his father, Cronus, who himself became lord of the universe after overthrowing his own father, Heaven. Cronus's inability to prevent his overthrow is the first example we see of the inevitability of fate—a recurring theme in mythological stories. Even Zeus himself is fated to be overthrown by one who is yet unborn.

Zeus attempts to learn the identity of his future overthrower from Prometheus but continues his daily habit of revelry, sometimes at the expense of innocent mortals and other gods. Always conscious of what he sees as an insurmountable difference between gods and humans, he has no pity for mortals. It is perhaps this essential lack of sympathy that enables Zeus to toy with humans heartlessly, raping and ruining the lives of many women, who seem to exist only for his pleasure. Yet this behavior only represents one side of Zeus's character; the other, more evolved side is his role as the divine upholder of justice for both gods and humans.

## Odysseus

Odysseus, king of Ithaca, is one of the best-known ancient Greek heroes. Homer's *Iliad* and Virgil's *Aeneid* both portray Odysseus as, if not the strongest Greek chieftain in the Trojan War, certainly the smartest and likely the most valuable. He is entrusted with any task that requires more than brute force, from drawing the great Achilles into the Greek army to inventing the tactic of the Trojan Horse—the ruse that finally enabled the Greeks to win the war. Odysseus's sharp wit works wonders that no feat of arms can achieve. It is in reflection of this worth that Odysseus is given the fallen Achilles' armor, the highest honor for a warrior.

Homer's other epic, the *Odyssey,* records Odysseus's journey back to Ithaca from Troy. It is the first—and until the *Aeneid,* the only—large-scale classical work focusing on one character. As such, Homer gives Odysseus a depth of character and richness of psychological texture lacking in other classical protagonists. Without supernatural powers or divine heritage, Odysseus must rely on his own shrewd intellect to survive—a human and modern approach to the challenges and temptations he encounters.

## OEDIPUS

Oedipus is remembered today largely in the context of the psychoanalytic theory of Sigmund Freud, as the mythic archetype of the allegedly universal psychic phenomenon that men unconsciously desire to kill their fathers and have sexual relations with their mothers. Regardless of the validity of Freud's theory, it is important to note that the theory does not provide a wholly accurate description of the Oedipus of classical mythology. Indeed, Oedipus does end up killing his father and marrying his mother, but he does so entirely without awareness. It is interesting that Freud looks to Oedipus as an incarnation of a supposedly universal trait, as there is indeed much in the story of Oedipus that makes him resonate in universal ways. First, and most apparent, is the case of the riddle of the Sphinx, which Oedipus solves at the gates of Thebes. The Sphinx asks which creature walks on four feet in the morning, two at noon, and three in the evening. Oedipus's answer is man, because man crawls as a baby, walks upright in maturity, and walks with a cane in old age. Perhaps the most direct and universal statement on the nature of man to be found in classical myth, this riddle retains its accuracy even today and still lies within our own power to answer.

Oedipus's subtler universality is evident later, when he learns the incredible truth about his mother and father. In despair, he puts out his own eyes and leaves his city to wander and eventually die. This form of self-punishment is an unusual choice: while we imagine he might choose to kill himself like his mother or the Sphinx have, his choice to blind himself is a poignant statement on the human condition. In putting out his eyes, Oedipus creates an actual, physical manifestation of what he understands his condition as a human being to be—that we are often blind to our true fate and, as a result, do not know the consequences of our actions. Oedipus thus also acknowledges that fate guides our steps from birth to death, brooding over us however or wherever we wander through life.

## Medea

Though Medea is generally less popular than some of the major male heroes of classical mythology, her story retains remarkable poignancy to this day. A princess from Colchis on the Black Sea, she first appears during the tale of Jason, a prince of Greece whose life she saves and for whom she secures the Golden Fleece, the object of his quest. After living with Medea as his wife for several years, Jason cruelly abandons her. Rather than meekly accept this wrong, Medea takes full vengeance on Jason—though at a terrible cost to herself—by killing his new bride and father-in-law, as well as the two small children she and Jason had together. Medea then rides off in a chariot drawn by dragons, which she is able to do because she is both a sorceress and a descendent of a god.

Medea is arguably the strongest non-Olympian woman in all of Greek mythology. There are many other wronged women in these myths: Dido and Ariadne, like Medea, sacrifice much to benefit their lovers and are also abandoned, while scores of other women are seduced or raped by the gods. However, many of the other female non-deities are either vain and jealous (Cassiopeia, the wicked stepmother Ino, and Hercules' wife Deianira) or stupid, calm, and voicelessly beautiful (Helen, who more closely resembles a snow-white heifer than a person). Though it is Jason who openly breaks his oath to the gods by promising fidelity to Medea, it is she who is demonized by classical tradition, with its condemning portrayal of her murderous act and her unremorseful flight from Earth. The reason for this is unclear, as it appears more complex than simple gender inequity. Medea represents certain aspects of culture that Greek society repressed: first, she is a "barbarian," from part of the vilified non-Greek world; and second, she is a witch and, as such, belongs to an earlier universe of religious beliefs and superstitions that were replaced by the Greek worldview. Even these considerations, however, do not entirely explain Medea's nature or the reception she receives—which is perhaps why, even today, her complicated, wounded, and misunderstood character remains a subject of fascination.

# Themes, Motifs & Symbols

## Themes

*Themes are the fundamental and often universal ideas explored in a literary work.*

### The Dominance of Fate

Fate was of great concern to the Greeks, and its workings resonate through many of their myths and texts. We see countless characters who go to great lengths in attempts to alter fate, even if they know such an aim to be futile. The inability of any mortal or immortal to change prescribed outcomes stems from the three Fates: sisters Clotho, who spins the thread of life; Lachesis, who assigns each person's destiny; and Atropos, who carries the scissors to snip the thread of life at its end. These three divinities pervade all the stories of Greek myth, whether they be stories of gods, goddesses, demigods, heroes, or mortals and regardless of the exploits recounted. Nothing can be done to alter or prolong the destiny of one's life, regardless of the number of preparations or precautions taken. This inflexibility applies just as much to Zeus as to the lowliest mortal, as we see in Zeus's hounding of Prometheus to divulge the name of the woman who will bear the offspring that one day will kill him.

Though this lesson is somewhat consoling—the way of the world cannot be bent to match the whims of those in authority—it is also very disturbing. The prospect of free will seems rather remote, and even acts of great valor and bravery seem completely useless. The myths provide an interesting counterpoint to this uselessness, however. In virtually all the stories in which a character does everything in his power to block a negative fate, and yet falls prey to it, we see that his efforts to subvert fate typically provide exactly the circumstances required for the prescribed fate to arise. In other words, the resisting characters themselves provide the path to fate's fulfillment.

A perfect example is the king of Thebes, who has learned that his son, Oedipus, will one day kill him. The king takes steps to ensure Oedipus's death but ends up ensuring only that he and Oedipus fail to recognize each other when they meet on the road many years later. This lack of recognition enables a dispute in which Oedipus slays his father without thinking twice. It is the king's exercise of free will, then, that ironically binds him even more surely to the thread of destiny. This mysterious, inexplicable twinning between will and fate is visible in many the stories and philosophical treatises of the Greeks.

## BLOODSHED BEGETS BLOODSHED

Aeschylus's *Oresteia,* Sophocles' *Oedipus* trilogy, Euripides' plays, and Homer's two great epics all demonstrate the irreparable persistence of bloodshed within Greek mythology that leads to death upon death. The royal house of Atreus is most marked in this regard: the house's ancestor, Tantalus, inexplicably cooks up his child and serves him to the gods, offending the deities and cursing the entire house with the spilling of its blood from generation to generation. We see the curse manifest when Atreus himself kills his brother's son and serves him up—an act of vengeance for wrong-doing done to him. Atreus's son, Agamemnon, then sacrifices his own daughter, Iphigenia, as he has been told it will procure good sailing winds for the Greeks to start off to Troy. Rather, this deed leads his wife, Clytemnestra, to kill him on his first night home, with support from his cousin Aegisthus, who is in turn avenging Atreus's crimes. Last but not least, Orestes, the son of Agamemnon and Clytemnestra, comes back to kill his mother and Aegisthus. Only two members remain in the House of Atreus: Orestes and his sister Electra. Everyone else has been foully murdered in this bloody chain of events.

Though these characters have brought terrible violence upon those to whom they owed bonds of love and loyalty, they are still not wholly condemnable. Orestes knows that he will incur the wrath of the Furies and the gods in committing matricide. As terrible as matricide is, Orestes would be even more in the wrong if he let his father's death go unpunished. Clytemnestra no doubt follows a similar rationale, as she cannot allow Agamemnon's sacrifice of their daughter to stand unavenged. Even this is not the beginning of the chain: Agamemnon felt he had no choice but to sacrifice Iphigenia, since his only other option was to break the oath he made to Menelaus years before. Indeed, the whole line of Atreus is cursed with such irresolvable dilemmas, the outcome of divine anger at Tantalus's horrific and unprompted sacrifice of his son. In this slippery world of confusing and conflicting ethics, the only certainty is that bloodshed merely begets more bloodshed.

## The Danger of Arrogance and Hubris

In many myths, mortals who display arrogance and hubris end up learning, in quite brutal ways, the folly of this overexertion of ego. The Greek concept of hubris refers to the overweening pride of humans who hold themselves up as equals to the gods. Hubris is one of the worst traits one can exhibit in the world of ancient Greece and invariably brings the worst kind of destruction.

The story of Niobe is a prime example of the danger of arrogance. Niobe has the audacity to compare herself to Leto, the mother of Artemis and Apollo, thus elevating herself and her children to the level of the divine. Insulted, the two gods strike all of Niobe's children dead and turn her into a rock that perpetually weeps. Likewise, young Phaëthon, who pridefully believes he can drive the chariot of his father, the Sun, loses control and burns everything in sight before Zeus knocks him from the sky with a thunderbolt. Similar warnings against hubris are found in the stories of Bellerophon, who bridles the winged Pegasus and tries to ride up to Olympus and join the deities' revelry, and Arachne, who challenges Athena to a weaving contest and is changed into a spider as punishment. Indeed, any type of hubris or arrogance, no matter the circumstance, is an attitude that no god will leave unpunished.

## Reward for Goodness and Retribution for Evil

The Greeks and Romans incorporated aspects of their ethical codes in their myths. In a sense, these stories are manuals of morality, providing models for correct conduct with examples of which behaviors are rewarded and which are punished. The clearest example is the story of Baucis and Philemon, an impoverished old couple who show kindness to the disguised Jupiter and Mercury. Of everyone in the city, only Baucis and Philemon are generous with their humble hospitality. Jupiter and Mercury reward them and destroy all the other inhabitants of the area. The lesson is clear: the gods judge our moral actions and dispense blessings or curses accordingly.

The idea of these myths as moral guides is not unlike the Judeo-Christian morality tales in the Bible. However, while the God of the Bible is an infallible moral authority, the gods who judge good and evil in classical myth harbor their own flaws. They have favorites and enemies, often for vain reasons—Hera's jealousy, for example, predisposes her against several entirely innocent women—and are capable of switching sides or abandoning their favorites for no clear reason, as Apollo does to Hector just as Hector faces Achilles in combat. Aside from their prejudices, of course, the gods are poor moral judges because they frequently act immorally themselves, philandering, raping, lying, and callously using innocent mortals as pawns.

## Motifs

*Motifs are recurring structures, contrasts, and literary devices that can help to develop and inform the text's major themes.*

### The Hero's Quest

The story of a hero with a quest frequently recurs in mythology. Many of these stories are similar: a hero is born, raised in poverty by foster parents or a single mother, and at a certain age ventures forth to reclaim his patrimony. He is charged with some very difficult task and is offered the hand of a noble woman in marriage upon his success. By accomplishing these tasks, the otherwise unknown hero demonstrates his fitness to take on his father's throne. This framework is subject to some degree of variation, of course, but it holds true for many of the hero stories Hamilton retells in *Mythology*.

Theseus is the perfect example: though raised far from Athens, he proves himself—from the moment he departs toward his father—a decent and upstanding heir by ridding the highway of bandits. Perseus, Hercules, Achilles, and others offer small variations on this framework of the hero's quest. Interestingly, however, Odysseus, whose name has come to be synonymous with the hero and quest, offers a notable difference from the archetype. He does not grow up away from his parents, and he is already married and undergoes an arduous journey on his return home after battle. This difference, perhaps, explains why Odysseus strongly resonates as a more modern character relevant to present times.

### Beauty

Beauty in all its forms figures prominently in Hamilton's *Mythology*, particularly in the Greek myths, which ascribe an immeasurable value to beauty. Though appreciation of beauty is hardly a surprising find, it may seem superficial to see aesthetic and artistic beauty given such a prominent place in myths that also purport to be religious or moral guides.

Nonetheless, the assertion that beautiful is better pervades the myths. It is evident in Zeus's and Apollo's philandering, Orpheus's winning over of Hades with his lovely music, the sparking of the

Trojan War over Helen's legendary loveliness, and Hera's and Athena's bitterness at Paris's preference for Aphrodite's fairness. With these myths in mind, we see that, in the classical worldview, beauty is not in the eye of the beholder, but rather a verifiable, objective actuality about which even the gods must agree.

### Love

The seemingly indefinable notion of love is an important agent in much of *Mythology,* the source for many rewards, punishments, motivations, and deceptions. The myths treat love in a way that is different from most of our modern-day ideas of love. In creation myths, love is described as a force, and it is out of love that Earth arises. There are actually very few ordinary love stories, at least in our traditional sense of the word, with a man and woman bonding in romance and living happily ever after. There are, rather, several tragic tales, as those of Pyramus and Thisbe or Ceyx and Alcyone, as well as many stories of unrequited love, such as Polyphemus and Galatea or Echo and Narcissus.

Broadening the myth's exploration of love and lust are tales of kidnapping and rape, such as Hades and Persephone or Apollo and Creusa. There are instances in which one party—always the woman—loves so strongly and under such false premises that it spells disaster for her. Such are the cases of Medea, Ariadne, and Dido, all of whom give themselves over to love, heart and soul—betraying their own families—only to have the men whom they love heartlessly move on after the women's usefulness is expended. These tales perhaps imply a cautionary warning that blood is thicker than water and that a bride's family by marriage is never as trustworthy as her birth family, to whom she truly owes allegiance.

## Symbols

*Symbols are objects, characters, figures, and colors used to represent abstract ideas or concepts.*

### Cannibalism

Cannibalism, eating the flesh of one's own kind, is disturbingly present in *Mythology.* While it might seem repulsive to include cannibalistic details within a story, there are a strikingly large number of myths in which people—for the most part children—are sliced, cooked, and eaten. Aside from Tantalus's inexplicably poor decision to serve his son to the gods, we see several stories in which the cannibalism of one's children serves as the sweetest revenge—as Atreus exacts it upon his brother, and Procne upon her husband, Tereus. Even Cronus, the father of Zeus and lord of the universe, methodically swallows his children one by one in an attempt to forestall his downfall. Though the prevalence of cannibalism in these myths might lead us to believe that the practice was accepted in classical society, we see that cannibalism is severely punished in each case. Why it occurs so frequently in the first place remains a mystery.

Perhaps the roots of cannibalism lie in human sacrifice, the same source Hamilton identifies in the flower myths of Hyacinth and Adonis. As we see, these sacrifices are unwanted by the gods and typically punished severely, an indictment of both cannibalism and human sacrifice. In this regard, it is interesting to note the one instance in which a god actually *does* want such a sacrifice: Artemis's call for the sacrifice of Iphigenia. Significantly, in a later telling of this myth, Artemis miraculously saves the girl instead.

ART

As civilizations prized for their art, it is no wonder that the Greeks and Romans retained a mythology that elevates art to a divine practice or at least one that almost consistently pleases the divine. The most prominent examples of mythological artistry are Pygmalion's beloved statue Galatea, Arachne's tapestry, and the poet who is the one person Odysseus spares from death at the end of the *Odyssey*. Both gods and mortals in the myths understand the power and influence of art almost as they do the unwritten rules of fate.

On a literary level, the symbol of art serves a glorifying purpose, staking a claim for the power of the text itself. This self-glorification is perhaps most obvious in Homer: Odysseus spares the poet, unlike the priest whom he has just dispatched, because he is loath to kill "such a man, taught by the gods to sing divinely." In a less than subtle way, Homer is hinting that he himself is one such sacred, divinely touched creature. In addition to this self-glorification, art is used to link men with their gods, as the gods not only appreciate art, but actually make it themselves. Apollo is proud of his lyre, Pan of his set of pipes, and Hephaestus of the artisanship of the fine products of his smithy. Art, then, is symbolically and literally a bridge between mortals and gods.

# Summary & Analysis

## Introduction to Classical Mythology

### Summary

Hamilton begins by highlighting the common misunderstanding that mythology depicts the blissful state of man in his original harmony with nature. On the contrary, Hamilton notes, the lives of ancient people were not romantic and beautiful, but full of hardship, disease, and violence. For Hamilton, the Greek myths are remarkable in that they show how far the Greeks, an ancient civilization, had advanced beyond a primitive state of savagery and brutality. By the time Homer wrote his epic, the *Iliad*, a new way of looking at the world had come into being. According to Hamilton, this new perspective is critically important, revealing a great deal not only about ancient Greece but about modern America as well—as so much of our own culture comes directly from the Greeks.

One of the most important aspects of the Greek worldview was that it was the first to put humans at the center of the universe. Unlike the animal deities of the Egyptians and Mesopotamians, the gods of the Greeks are human in form. Not only do they possess human physical characteristics, but they embody the emotional flaws of humans as well. Unlike the gods of other ancient civilizations, Greek gods are not infinitely omniscient and omnipotent, manifesting typical human foibles such as philandering, feasting and drinking, and obsessive jealousy. To the Greeks, the life of the gods so closely resembled human life that the gods felt real and tangible, rather than incomprehensible and remote.

In this way, Hamilton argues, the myths of the Greeks reflect a view of the universe that acknowledges the mystery and beauty of humanity. Even the most magical of Greek myths contain real-world elements: the supernatural Hercules lives in the very real city of Thebes, and the goddess Aphrodite is born in a spot any ancient tourist could visit, off the island of Cythera. In general, Greek myths involve less strange and frightening magic than the myths of other ancient civilizations. In this more rational world, individuals become heroes by virtue of bravery and strength rather than supernatural powers. Hamilton contends that this revolutionary way of thinking about the world elevates humans and the worth of their abilities, making it a far less terrifying place in which to live.

Hamilton points out a downside to this rational view of the supernatural—like humans, the gods are often unpredictable. They do not always operate on the highest moral grounds, and they get angry and jealous, sometimes doing terrible things like exacting vengeance or calling for sacrifices. Even though Greek myth lacks wizards and demonic spellcasters, there are still plenty of horrible magic creatures—the snake-haired Gorgons, for instance—that appear to be relics of that older, primitive world. In the end, however, as Hamilton points out, the Greek hero always manages to defeat these creatures.

At the same time, Hamilton reminds us that these myths do not really constitute the religion of the Greeks. These myths are more akin to proto-scientific stories that are meant to explain natural phenomena, such as thunderstorms or the setting of the sun. Some myths are pure entertainment and are not meant to explain anything. On the whole, the later myths appear more religious, as Zeus, the primary god, begins to resemble the sort of omnipotent God-figure familiar to modern readers—in the *Iliad*, he is very human and moody, but by the *Odyssey* he is more wise and compassionate. Zeus changes so much from the old philanderer he once was that he begins to look very much like the Judeo-Christian concept of God.

Having traced the origins, characters, and changes over time of the content of the myths, Hamilton now tackles their literary record. In this book, she explains, she has compiled myths from a wide variety of sources. The Roman poet Ovid is an especially important source, as he recorded more of the myths than anyone else, and many of the tales we have now have only survived as result of his efforts. However, Hamilton says she has tried to use Ovid as sparingly as possible because, as he appeared so late in the game, and he did not believe in the myths he was writing and merely treated them as tales. Homer, in contrast, is the earliest known Greek poet, and Hesiod, who lived in the eighth or ninth century B.C., is another very early source. Hesiod was a poor farmer, and his myths reflect his deep religious piety and the harshness of his life. Chronologically, the next source is the cycle of Homeric Hymns, though Hamilton never uses them outright in her text. The earliest Hymn was written in the seventh or eighth century B.C., and the latest in the fourth or fifth century B.C. Pindar, at the end of the sixth century B.C., was the greatest lyric poet of Greece, while Aeschylus, Sophocles, and

Euripides were three famous tragic playwrights from the sixth and fifth centuries B.C. Next, Apollonius of Rhodes—important for his epic about the hero Jason—and Apollodorus, whose writing dates from the first or second century A.D., are the last two Greek writers Hamilton studies. Among the Roman authors who wrote their own versions of the original Greek myths, Virgil is most notable. Though, like his contemporary Ovid, he did not believe the myths as religious truth; he treated them seriously, seeing the important humanity at their cores.

## Analysis

Hamilton's personal opinions, which come to the forefront here, are largely submerged throughout the rest of the text, as she only plays the role of collector or interpreter. Here, however, she explicitly states her theory of myths. To a modern reader, some of it may seem strange and dated, as Hamilton's assumption of a single strand of human history—proceeding neatly from "primitive" man to the Greeks and from the Greeks to "us"—is heavily Eurocentric in comparison with the multiculturalism of today. This mode of imperialist or colonialist philosophy was popular at the time Hamilton was writing. The idea that there is a single standard of civilization— European—and that all other societies are barbaric has been discredited by the work of scholars in the intervening decades.

Hamilton's explanations of the nature of myths also reflect her historical moment: while it may have made good sense then ("according to the most modern idea," she says) to categorize myths as either primitive science or simple entertainment, scholars today have a more sophisticated understanding of the role of myth in culture. At times, Hamilton seems to be stretching a little, exaggerating in order to better fit her theories. She writes, for example, that Greek heroes rarely wield magic and that the mythical universe is highly rational—claims that are suspect in light of elements such as Hercules' superhuman strength, Perseus's magic flying shoes, and Odysseus's visit to the land of the dead. Yet Hamilton must make these claims in order to support her argument that Greek myths reflect a more rational, cultivated, and advanced society in comparison with others. Hamilton also stretches a bit with her theories about the development of Greek religion. Like a missionary of the colonial era, she implies that the Judeo-Christian God is a necessary part of the truly civilized society. Arguing that Zeus evolved over time into a universal father figure, she implies that classical civilization became more "civilized" as time went on—an idea essential to her notion of history as a progression from primitivism to advancement. Such an evolution is not really supported by the myths she records, however, as Zeus remains a philanderer, acting foolishly, capriciously, and even cruelly to the end. Perhaps Hamilton's theory is indeed valid, but her text does not support it with evidence.

Though Hamilton's account may be reductively exclusive of anything contrary to her theory, she does make several excellent points about the nature of the Greek worldview and its difference from the worldviews of other ancient civilizations. The fact that the Greek gods had human forms is significant and does likely reflect the rationality of Greek society—though the Greeks were not the first or only ancient people to have them, as the early Hindus had a similar cast of divinities. Hamilton is also quite right in her observation that our own culture, even today, owes much to the Greeks, as words like *democracy* and *philosophy* attest. These myths, then, give us a window into a culture very important for understanding not only its moment and our moment, but all the years of Western history between. Though the myths' religious and scientific appeal has faded for us, they are still beautiful, complex, and engaging stories that speak volumes about our cultural ancestors and ourselves—in ways so powerful that, as they did for Hamilton, defy explanation.

# Part One, Chapters I–II

### Summary: Chapter I — The Gods

Unlike many other creation stories, in the Greek versions the gods are created *by* the universe instead of the other way around. In the beginning, two entities exist, Heaven and Earth. Their children are the Titans, whose children, in turn, are the Olympians, the main Greek gods. The Titans—who include such notables as Ocean, Mnemosyne (Memory), and Prometheus, mankind's benefactor—rule the universe until Zeus and their other children conquer them.

The term "Olympians" comes from Mount Olympus, the gods' mystical home, which is conceived as a high mountaintop but is really a magical place that exists on a heavenly plane—not the heavens (which Zeus alone rules), earth, sea, nor underworld. Shared by all the gods, Olympus is perfect. Rain never falls there, and the gods while away their time eating, drinking, and listening to music. There are twelve proper Olympians: Zeus; his two brothers, Poseidon and Hades; his two sisters, Hestia and Hera (who is also his wife); his children, Ares, Athena, Apollo, Hermes, and Artemis; and two gods sometimes considered his offspring, Hephaestus and Aphrodite.

There are also lesser gods in Olympus, like Eros, the Graces, and the Muses. Several, like Hebe, goddess of Youth, are rarely mentioned in myths. There are also a few abstract forces personified, if not completely, who live on Olympus: Themis, Divine Justice; Dike, Human Justice; Nemesis, Righteous Anger; and Aidos, the sense of respect and shame that keeps humans from sinning.

Besides the Olympians, supernaturals also abound in the sea and underworld. Poseidon rules the sea, which is populated by the Nereids, sea nymphs who are distinct from the Naiads, the freshwater nymphs; Triton, the trumpeter of the sea; the shape-shifting Proteus, Poseidon's son or attendant; Pontus, a god of the deep sea; and Nereus, a god of the Mediterranean. There is a different god for every river, and the Titan Ocean—lord of the mysterious river that encircles the earth—lives there along with several other minor water gods.

Hades and his queen, Persephone, are the only rulers of the underworld—a place often simply referred to as Hades, after its king. A mysterious locale somewhere under the earth, it is the realm of the dead. Many myths concern a mortal's journey to the underworld and his encounters with its vicious guardian, the three-headed dog Cerberus. Divided into two sections, Tartarus and Erebus, Hades has five famous rivers: Acheron, the river of woe; Cocytus, the river of lamentation; Phlegethon, the river of fire; Styx, the river of the gods' unbreakable oath; and Lethe, the river of forgetfulness. A boatman named Charon ferries the dead from Erebus across the junction of the Acheron and the Cocytus to the gates of Tartarus, where they are judged by three former kings, Rhadamanthus, Minos, and Aeacus. The wicked are sentenced to eternal torment, while the good are admitted to the Elysian Fields, a place of perfect bliss. Other dwellers of Hades include the Furies and the personified forces of Sleep and Death.

Earth has its share of lesser gods as well. Pan and Silenus are mischievous and jovial earth gods. Pan rules over the Satyrs, a race of goat-men, and dances with the Dryads, the forest nymphs, and the Oreads, the mountain nymphs. Also on earth are the twins Castor and Pollux, sometimes spoken of as gods. The twins represent the ideal of brotherly devotion because, when an angry cattle-herder named Idas killed Castor, Pollux begged to die out of love for his brother. Rewarding this devotion, Zeus allows them to spend half the year in Hades and the other half on earth. Earth is also home to the wind gods: Aeolus, King of the Winds; Boreas, the North Wind; Zephyr, the West; Notus, the South; and Eurus, the East. The earth is also home to many other nondivine supernatural beings, such as the Centaurs—half-men, half-horses, one of whom is Chiron, an important tutor to many eventual heroes. Two trios of sisters are also earth-bound: the fearsome Gorgons, of which Medusa is one, and the Graiae, three ancients who share one eye. Finally, the Fates, who are assigned neither a place in heaven nor earth, spin, measure, and cut the threads of men's lives. The Fates are not subject to the decrees of any of the gods, not even Zeus himself.

With few meaningful changes, the Romans adopted much of Greek mythology, as their existing deities—the Numina, the Lares, and the Penates—were largely abstract, vague personifications of the processes of daily life. The most significant Numina were Janus and Saturn, who later represented the Greek Cronus, Zeus's father.

## Summary: Chapter II — The Two Great Gods of the Earth

Aside from the twelve Olympians, there are two equally important gods who reside on earth: Demeter and Dionysus (Bacchus). These two are the best friends of humanity: Demeter, goddess of the harvest and nature, provides fruitful plenty and protects the threshing-floor, while Dionysus, god of wine and revelry, rules the grapevine and so the production of wine. Demeter is celebrated in a festival every fifth September; her prime temple is at Eleusis, and her worship is a central and mysterious aspect of ancient life. Bacchus also comes to be worshipped at Eleusis—a natural pairing of the two gods who bring the pleasant gifts of the earth and, significantly, are both overpowered by seasonal change. Just as the frost kills the fields and the vines, these two gods—unlike the Olympians—live in a world filled with regular suffering.

Hades, wanting a queen, kidnaps Demeter's only child, Persephone. Demeter wanders the earth in aimless despair, eventually resting in Eleusis in human disguise. One day, the kind family that has been harboring her accidentally discovers her divine nature and offends her. They build the great temple at Eleusis to appease her anger. Still, Demeter locks herself in the temple out of sadness, and at that time nothing grows on the earth. Finally, Zeus sends Hermes down to Hades to try to set everything right. Hades agrees to let Persephone return to her mother but slyly makes her eat a magic pomegranate seed that necessitates her return. Eventually a compromise is arranged: Persephone will stay with Hades for one-third of the year, Demeter for the other two-thirds. When Persephone returns to the underworld at the start of each winter, Demeter's renewed sorrow makes the Earth barren. Persephone returns each spring, causing Demeter's joy and thus the springtime's blossoming.

Dionysus is the only main god who has one human parent: Zeus is his father, but his mother is a mortal named Semele. Enraged at Zeus's affair, Hera cunningly fixed Semele's death while she was pregnant. Zeus snatched the baby from his mother's burning body and implanted it in his own side until birth, when Hermes carried the infant god off to be raised in secrecy by the nymphs of Nysa, a magic valley. Dionysus is generally a good god, spreading the secrets of wine production everywhere he goes. He even loves the mortal Ariadne after Theseus cruelly abandons her and dares defy Hades and rescue his mother from death. Somehow succeeding, Dionysus leads Semele up to live as an immortal in Olympus. He has another side, however; as one might expect from the lord of wine, he is a god of madness and insanity. The wild, bloody Maenads are his followers. When Pentheus, king of Thebes, defies him, Dionysus drives Pentheus's mother and sisters so insane that they rip Pentheus apart with their bare hands. Dionysus is the final component of the Greek pantheon, and as time goes on, his influence grows. He eventually becomes the god of holy inspiration, in whose honor the most famous theater and poetry festival is held. Taking place every spring, it commemorates his rebirth—according to one story, he is torn to pieces each year either by the Titans or by Hera's orders, depending on the version of the myth. Like Demeter's, his story is one of tragedy and death, though he always rises from the dead.

## Analysis: Chapters I–II

Hamilton introduces the Greek gods as divine beings whose actions offer some preliminary explanations for the mysteries of the world and also shows us just how much the gods resemble humans. They sometimes make mistakes, fight with one another, and in some cases even suffer. This human aspect of the gods cements the link between the divine and the visible world and lends credibility to the explanations the myths set forth, implying that the uncertainty and mystery of nature that surrounds us could be explained by the erratic actions of the gods. So, if it was puzzling to the Greeks that wine could cause drunken happiness and inspiration but also lead to wild, dangerous madness, its duality is reconciled by the stories that depict the dual nature of Dionysus himself. That deeply perplexing condition of the seasons—fields mysteriously lie barren for a third of the year and then break out into beautiful, flowery spring—is accounted for by Demeter's annual mourning for the loss of her daughter. Dionysus's duplicity and Demeter's depression are two very human qualities and allow us to explain otherworldly phenomena with reference to the same characteristics we see in other people in the visible world.

As these myths play such a vital role in explaining the innumerable twists and peculiarities of the world, it is no surprise that there is such an enormous cast of characters. The realm of waterways and navigation alone warrants a whole cast of characters in itself. Seafaring and sea trade were critically important to Greek civilization, so the Greeks felt a need to explain the complexities of bodies of water—hence the wide variety of water-oriented gods. The tumult of the seas and rivers can be explained by the warring wishes of their respective gods, just as a stormy sea could signify the anger of Poseidon and a calm sea the beneficence of a sea-nymph. Since much of what occurs in the waters is inexplicable, the Greeks could not ascribe it all to one all-powerful water god, therefore a whole host of divinities were used to explain the wide variety of watery mysteries. The large number of gods and beings thus indicates the complexity the Greeks found in the world around them, which is reflected in the intricate, specific explanations provided by their myths.

The complexity of the myths and the large cast of characters may also be due to the diversity of sources and traditions from which Hamilton compiles her material. She borrows from playwrights and poets whose works span two vastly different cultures and more than a millennium of history. Versions of the same myths differ across these sources, as Greek and Roman cultures had no singular work—like the Bible in Judeo-Christian tradition—to house a definitive version of their stories. Each author was thus an independent inventor, altering the myths to suit his own tastes and purposes. Hamilton herself is a similar kind of reteller, a redefiner and reinterpreter more than a simple collector of stories. She notes multiple versions of her stories, but usually prefers one over others. In any case, her retelling alerts us to the incredible depth of the world of Greek myth.

# Part One, Chapters III–IV

## Summary: Chapter III — How the World and Mankind Were Created

As she does through the rest of the book, Hamilton begins the chapter with a note explaining and evaluating its sources—an important note, as the various sources can tell radically different stories. Chapter III comes mostly from Hesiod, one of the earliest Greek poets.

In the beginning of the universe there is only Chaos. Chaos somehow gives birth to two children, Night and Erebus (the primeval underworld) out of the swirling energy. Love is born from these two, who in turn gives birth to Light and Day. Earth appears; its creation is never explained, as it just emerges naturally out of Love, Light, and Day. Earth gives birth to Heaven. Father Heaven and Mother Earth then create all other life, first producing a host of terrible monsters—the one-eyed Cyclopes and creatures with a hundred hands and fifty heads. Then the Titans are born. One of them, Cronus, kills Father Heaven, and the Titans rule the universe. From the blood of Heaven spring both the Giants and the avenging Furies.

Next comes a dramatic coup. Powerful Cronus, learning that one of his children is fated to kill him, eats each one as he or she is born. His wife Rhea, upset, hides one baby by replacing it with a stone for Cronus to eat instead. This infant eventually grows up and becomes Zeus, who forces Cronus to vomit up his brothers and sisters. The siblings band together against the Titans. With the help of one sympathetic Titan, Prometheus, and the monsters whom the Titans had enslaved, Zeus and his siblings win. They chain up the Titans in the bowels of the earth, except for Prometheus and Epimetheus, his brother. Prometheus's other brother, Atlas, is sentenced to forever bear the weight of the world on his shoulders as punishment.

The Greeks viewed Earth as a round disk divided into equal parts by the Mediterranean (the Sea) and the Black Sea (first called the Unfriendly, then the Friendly Sea). Ocean, a mystical river, flowed around the entire disk, and mysterious peoples—the Hyperboreans in the north, the Ethiopians in the far south and the Cimmerians in parts unknown—lived outside Ocean's perimeter.

There are three stories about the creation of humankind. In one, wise Prometheus and his scatterbrained brother Epimetheus are put in charge of making humans. Epimetheus bungles the job and gives all the useful abilities to animals, but Prometheus gives humans the shape of the gods and then the most precious gift of all—fire, which he takes from heaven. Later, Prometheus helps men by tricking Zeus into accepting the worst parts of the animal as a sacrifice from men. Zeus tortures Prometheus to punish him for stealing fire and to intimidate him into telling a secret: the identity of the mother whose child will one day overthrow Zeus (as Zeus had Cronus). Zeus chains Prometheus to a rock in the Caucasus, and every day an eagle comes to tear at his insides. Prometheus never gives in, however.

In the second creation myth, the gods themselves make humans. They use metals, starting with the best but using ones of progressively worse quality. The first humans were gold and virtually perfect; the next were silver; then brass, each worse than the last. The humans now upon the earth are the gods' fifth and worst version yet—the iron race. Full of evil and wickedness, each successive generation worsens until, one day, Zeus will wipe it out. There is also an explanation for how the perfect creatures of the Golden Age grew wicked. Zeus, outraged at Prometheus's treachery in giving humans fire and helping them cheat the gods with their offers of sacrifice, decides to punish men. He creates Pandora, the first woman, who, like the biblical Eve, brings suffering upon humanity through her curiosity. The gods give Pandora a box and tell her never to open it. She foolishly does, however, allowing all the evils of the universe pent up inside to rush out. The one thing she manages to retain in the box is Hope, humans' only comfort in the face of misfortune.

The third creation myth also starts with humans fashioned out of inanimate material. This time, Zeus, angry at the wickedness of the world, sends a great flood to destroy it. Only two mortal beings survive: Prometheus's son, Deucalion, and Epithemeus and Pandora's daughter, Pyrrha. After the flood, a voice in a temple orders the two to walk about and cast stones behind them. These stones become the first ancestors of the humans now inhabiting the earth.

## Summary: Chapter IV — The Earliest Heroes

### *Prometheus and Io*

These next stories come from a wide variety of Greek and Roman sources. We pick up again with Prometheus, who, chained up in the Caucasus, has occasion to comfort a dazzling white heifer. It turns out to be no ordinary cow but a woman named Io whom the perpetually unfaithful Zeus has seduced and then transformed into a cow to hide his transgression from Hera. Not so easily deceived, Hera asks Zeus to give her the cow and then imprisons her. Hermes, sent by Zeus, frees Io. Hera retaliates by sending a gadfly to annoy Io endlessly, forcing her to wander all over the world. At last encountering Prometheus, weary Io learns she will soon be turned back into a human, will bear Zeus a son, through whom she will be the ancestress of Hercules—the hero who eventually frees Prometheus.

### *Europa*

Europa is another victim of Zeus's lust. He spies the lovely maiden in the fields one day and then transforms himself into a beautiful, friendly bull. Charmed, she climbs on the bull's back, but he suddenly becomes frenzied and charges over the sea. Taking Europa to Crete, away from Hera's watchful eye, Zeus returns to his form and seduces her. Her descendants include two of Hades' judges—Minos and Rhadamanthus—and the continent of Europe is named for her.

### The Cyclops Polyphemus
Another famous casualty of justice is Polyphemus, one of the Cyclopes, the one-eyed monsters who were the only original children of Earth not banished by the Olympians after their victory. They are also the forgers of Zeus's thunderbolts. Best known for his encounter with Odysseus, Polyphemus is also the victim of a tragic infatuation, as Galatea, the beautiful, cruel sea nymph, never returns his feelings.

### Flower-Myths: Narcissus, Hyacinth, Adonis
Several floral-origin myths tell how the narcissus, hyacinth, and blood-red anemone flowers came into being. There are two stories of the narcissus. In the first, Zeus creates it as a bait to help Hades kidnap Persephone. The second and more famous tale concerns a handsome young man named Narcissus. Self-obsessed, he constantly breaks the hearts of others enamored of his beauty, including the nymph Echo—who could only repeat what was said to her, hence the modern meaning of echo. Finally, the goddess Nemesis, who is the personification of righteous anger, punishes Narcissus, allowing him to love no one but himself. He dies gazing at his own face in a pool of water, unable to break free from the sight. The nymphs who have loved him, albeit unrequitedly, create a flower in his name.

The hyacinth is created when Apollo accidentally kills his dear friend Hyacinth with a discus (in another version, jealous Zephyr, the West Wind, caused it to strike Hyacinth). Apollo makes the flower as a remembrance of his companion. The red anemone has a similar story. Adonis—a youth so handsome that even the goddess of love, Aphrodite, is enamored—is loved by everyone who sees him. Persephone and Aphrodite share him until a boar gores him during a hunt. Adonis goes forever to Persephone's realm of the dead, and the red anemone springs up where his blood hit the earth.

### ANALYSIS: CHAPTERS III–IV
These stories establish the fundamentals of Greek civilization very broadly, but the details leave us a strangely incomplete picture of the origins of civilization. Phenomena that we understand in other ways find wholly different explanations. In Greek myth, the universe *creates* its own gods, while we are used to it happening the

other way around. Moreover, the Greeks consider the earth to be a flat disk surrounded by a river named Ocean, beyond which live strange, inaccessible peoples, rather than as a spherical globe that orbits a star.

Perhaps the most strikingly foreign elements in these stories are the violence, incest, and immorality that lie at their heart. Zeus kills his father Cronus, who himself has wounded his father Heaven gravely. Earth and Heaven have both a mother-son and husband-wife relationship, just as Zeus and Hera have both a brother-sister and husband-wife relationship. Zeus is cruel to Prometheus, just as Hera is cruel to the innocent women Zeus seduces. Meanwhile, humanity's lot is one of death, destruction, and inevitable doom at the hand of Zeus—who will himself one day be overthrown.

Hamilton believes that this sinister tone—found even in the flower myths—is a vestigial trace from an older tradition. She points out that, although human sacrifice was not a part of Greek culture when these myths were written down, the connection between human blood and the growth in the fields suggests an older time when such sacrifice was used to promote springtime growth. The constant pain, deceit, and violence of the myths are not merely relics, however, but also reflect aspects of real life in the ancient world. As wars were common and existence was difficult, it makes sense that even the divine members of this world mirror this hardship.

These early myths, however, also emphasize noble values. Perhaps most surprising is the central motif of love: despite the violence and darkness, love remains the primary and essential virtue of the myths—the inexplicable force at the center of the creation of Heaven and Earth. Love is constantly celebrated in the morals of the stories: Prometheus displays noble, selfless love for humanity; Zeus's crime against his father is forgivable because he is acting out of filial love and obedience; Apollo's love for Hyacinth and Aphrodite's love for Adonis create beautiful flowers out of their lovers' blood; and Zeus's indiscretions can be interpreted as more than mere maliciousness because they come out of love, not a desire to cause further rupture with his wife. Perhaps most telling of all, the cruel punishment given to Narcissus is his incapacity to really love anybody. Love is important because it inspires kindness and trust—the moral foundation upon which Greek civilization rests.

Another value stressed here is justified rebellion against unjust authority. Prometheus embodies this virtue, defying Zeus repeatedly to help mankind, even in the face of terrible torture. Zeus himself defies his father in the face of injustice. Violence is a constant in the world, but the myths help make sense of it by drawing the distinction between cruel violence and justified violence. As we can see, justified violence often results in rewards—as Zeus becomes ruler of the Heavens—while cruel violence only begets retribution.

These hallmarks—love, trust, the glory of rebellion against unjust authority, and the idea of reward for upright actions and retribution for evil—form the core of the myth's moral element. The Greeks used these myths to guide their actions, separating good from evil, what pleases the gods from what displeases them, what results in fortune from what results in misfortune. Yet a stranger, subtler role of fate also braids itself into this pattern. Time and again, the gods and other supernatural beings try to thwart their fates and fail. Cronus's attempt to prevent his overthrow only plants the very seed that ensures that downfall, making Rhea so miserable that she saves Zeus, who subsequently kills Cronus. These themes—which come up again and again in the stories to come, most notably in the story of Oedipus—reflect the ancient Greeks' puzzlement over the workings of the world and the reason that good deeds sometimes reap unhappiness. In these myths, then, we see the groping for answers that perhaps introduced the Greeks to philosophy.

## Part Two, Chapters I–II

### Summary: Chapter I — Cupid and Psyche

Hamilton draws this story from the Latin writer Apuleius, who, like Ovid, was interested in creating beautiful, entertaining tales—a style that could not be further from Hesiod's pious, fearsome creation stories. Appealing to the Roman aesthetic sense, Apuleius's protagonist is Psyche, a princess so beautiful that men begin to worship her instead of Venus (the Latin name for Aphrodite). Insulted, Venus sends her son, Cupid (Latin name for Eros), to make Psyche fall in love with the ugliest creature in the world. Cupid, however, falls in love with her himself and magically prevents anyone else from doing so. Apollo convinces Psyche's father to leave her at the top of a hill to be wed to a monster. However, Zephyr, the West Wind, carries the waiting Psyche to a majestic palace where she bathes and feasts royally, attended by mysterious voices. At night, she feels a man next to her who introduces himself as her husband.

For a while, a pattern develops where Psyche remains alone during the day and then at night sleeps with a husband she never sees. She at last convinces the mysterious man to allow her sisters to visit her, even though he warns her it will end in tragedy. Psyche's sisters, jealous of her palace, conspire to ruin her marriage. Knowing she has never seen her husband, they slyly plant the idea in her head that he is a horrendous monster. Plagued by doubt, Psyche decides she must see what he looks like and, if he is a monster, stab him through his heart. That night, she lights a lamp and sees that her husband is the unbelievably beautiful Cupid. Psyche's hands tremble, spilling hot oil from the lamp and burning the god, revealing her deception. Cupid flees the house and runs to Venus to heal his wound.

Crushed, Psyche goes to Venus's home to see Cupid. Venus, enraged that Psyche has once again defied her, forces her to perform four seemingly impossible tasks. First, she must sort an enormous mound of seeds in one evening, but ants come to her aid and she succeeds. Second, she must fetch the golden wool of a flock of vicious wild sheep, but a reed by the riverbank tells her where to find wool that the sheep had snagged on thorns. Third, she must fill a flask with water from a treacherous waterfall of the river Styx, but an eagle swoops down and fills it for her. Finally, Psyche must journey to the underworld and convince Proserpine (Latin Persephone) to place some of her beauty in a box, but a tower on the way speaks to her and tells her how to easily complete the task.

On the way back from this final task, Psyche's curiosity makes her peek into the box to see what Proserpine's beauty looks like. The box appears empty, but a deep sleep overcomes her. Finally healed, Cupid rushes to her, and he then convinces Jupiter (Latin Zeus) to make her an immortal, which at last persuades Venus to accept her.

## Summary: Chapter II — Eight Brief Tales of Lovers

### *Pyramus and Thisbe*
Not all tales of love end so happily, as we see in Ovid's tale of Pyramus and Thisbe. The two lovers reside in Babylon, but their parents hate each other and forbid their marriage. Talking through a crack in the wall of the building their families share, they eventually decide to elope, agreeing to meet outside the city walls at a well-known mulberry tree. Thisbe gets there first but flees when she sees a lioness, intending to come back later. But she drops her cloak, and Pyramus, finding it bloody and torn by the lion, thinks she has been killed by the lion. Pyramus kills himself, covering the white berries of the mulberry tree with blood. Returning to find him dead, Thisbe then kills herself with his sword. The berries of the mulberry tree have forever stayed red to commemorate the tragic end of their love story.

### Orpheus and Eurydice

The next tale introduces Orpheus, the son of one of the Muses and the greatest mortal musician. Orpheus's music moves any human, god, animal, or object that hears it. His wife Eurydice is killed by a snake, and his music enables him to safely make the perilous journey to the underworld and convince Pluto (Hades) to let Eurydice return to the world of the living. The one catch to Eurydice's return is that she must walk behind Orpheus on the way back to earth; if he turns to look at her, she must return to Hades forever. Overcome with desire and doubt, Orpheus turns around too soon. Having lost Eurydice, he wanders aimlessly and gets ripped to shreds by Maenads.

### Ceyx and Alcyone

Ceyx is a king of Thessaly, and Alcyone is his loving wife. He sets out on a long journey, and his wife prays to the gods, particularly Juno, to protect him. Ceyx's ship unfortunately has already been wrecked in a storm, but Juno, pitying Alcyone, sends her a dream in which Ceyx tells what befell him. Alcyone wakes and rushes to the seashore, finding his body borne in on the tide. The gods transform her into a bird and also resurrect Ceyx as a bird, out of respect for their love. These two fly together eternally, and the phrase "halcyon days" comes from Alcyone, referring to the seven days a year when she calms the seas in order to lay her eggs on its smooth surface.

### Pygmalion and Galatea

Pygmalion, a sculptor, hates women and finds comfort only in his art. One day he makes a statue of a woman so beautiful that he falls in love with it. Intrigued by this new kind of love, Venus rewards him by bringing the statue to life. Pygmalion names her Galatea. Their son, Paphos, lends his name to Venus's favorite city.

### Baucis and Philemon

The love of Baucis and Philemon is also rewarded by the gods. One day, Jupiter and Mercury (Latin Hermes) descend to earth in disguise in order to test the hospitality of the people of Phrygia. No one is kind to them except an old couple, Baucis and Philemon, who are very poor. Revealing themselves, Jupiter and Mercury drown the rest of Phrygia's wicked inhabitants in a flood and offer Baucis and Philemon any wish they desire. Modest and content, Baucis and Philemon merely ask never to live apart from one another. The two thus live to a very old age, when the gods transform them into two trees—a linden and an oak—growing out of a single trunk.

## *Endymion and Daphne*
Though they are not lovers to each other, Endymion and Daphne each have an important relation to an immortal. Endymion is a handsome young shepherd loved by Selene, the Moon, who casts a magic sleep over him so that she can visit him whenever she wants. She is always sad, however, as he can never return her love. Daphne is a beautiful, headstrong huntress-nymph whom Apollo loves. She runs away from him but he pursues her all the way to the waters of her father, the river god Peneus. Appealing for instant help, Daphne finds her arms hardening and twisting—her father turns her into a laurel tree. Apollo proclaims that the laurel will forever be his sacred tree, and, since that time, its leaves signify music, songs, and triumphs.

## *Alpheus and Arethusa*
Arethusa is another huntress who disdains marriage and is also pursued by a god—the river god Alpheus. When he is about to overtake her, she appeals to Artemis for help. Changed into a spring of water, Arethusa plunges deep into the earth. Alpheus changes himself into a river, and their waters mingle, forming a connection between the river Alpheus in Greece and Arethusa's spring in Sicily.

## ANALYSIS: CHAPTERS I–II
The different styles of Hamilton's sources are apparent in these chapters. Except for the story of Endymion—which, written by the Greek Theocritus, does indeed stand out as unique—these tales all come from Latin writers, primarily Ovid. We must remember that the earliest Greek myths date from about 1000 B.C. and Hesiod's creation stories from about 700 B.C. At this time, Greece was a violent, unstable set of city-states. Its authors faced a virtual literary void, as no one had gone before to explain the incomprehensible mysteries of life. The world of the Latin writers were very different, as many characterize the Roman world as an even more secure, luxurious, and ordered world than our own today. Rome was the largest empire known to man, and wealth and luxury abounded to the point of decadence. Light, gaudy tales of lovers were in demand, since the Romans preferred pretty accompaniments to aristocratic banquets rather than dread epics of the beginning of the world or humbling accounts of man's modest origins.

These stories must be read in the context of such a cultural moment. Though details of Roman life are not the subject at hand, they are important to making sense of the themes of these myths and evaluating their place in the larger realm of classical mythology. Clearly, the force of love—an important force in Hesiod's account of the creation—is given further weight here. Cupid, burnt by Psyche's oil, cries out, "Love cannot live where there is no trust." True love is always rewarded, even if it meets a tragic end: Pyramus and Thisbe are forever remembered by the red mulberries, and the Muses celebrate Orpheus by burying him at the foot of Mount Olympus.

The place of women in these stories deserves some scrutiny. The myths reflect the patriarchal structure of classical civilization in a variety of ways. Though, to us, Psyche's desire to see her husband's face is wholly understandable, she is punished nonetheless. Daphne and Arethusa, who despise marriage for the loss of independence it entails, are pursued against their will. As we have seen in the story of Pandora, classical society saw women as inferior to men and an inherent cause of evil. Nonetheless, there are numerous powerful goddesses in the Greek pantheon: Hera, who often outwits and punishes Zeus; the strong and independent Athena and Artemis; the revered Demeter; and the Fates—perhaps the most powerful beings of all—are all female, complicating the myths' patriarchal tone.

Another major virtue that makes up the myths' moral guidance is obedience. Psyche's troubles stem from her disobedience of Cupid, just as Daphne's and Arethusa's stem from their resistance of divine lovers. Considering the gods' occasional impulsiveness and irrationality, we may question why the Greeks felt that obedience to such capricious will was so important. Perhaps this sense of divine power and purpose gave the Greeks a sense of security, a sense that the world was less chaotic. Indeed, despite their shortcomings, the gods generally do reward the good and punish the evil, thus making sense of right and wrong. Obedience to the gods not only indicates acceptance of the world as it is, but also acceptance of the moral code of the society, critically important in a fiercely democratic culture.

## Part Two, Chapters III–IV

### Summary: Chapter III — The Quest of the Golden Fleece

Hamilton's account of the Golden Fleece comes from Apollonius of Rhodes, a Greek poet from about 300 B.C. Athamas, a king, gets tired of his first wife, Nephele, and marries a second, Ino. Ino wants Nephele's son, Phrixus, out of the way so her own son can inherit the throne. Hermes sends a flying golden ram to rescue Phrixus and his sister, Helle, who falls off the ram and dies. Phrixus safely reaches the land of Colchis, where he sacrifices the ram to Zeus and gives its skin—the Golden Fleece—to Colchis's king, Aetes.

Meanwhile, a man named Pelias has usurped the throne of Phrixus's uncle, a Greek king. Jason, the deposed king's son, grows up and returns to reclaim the throne. En route to Pelias's kingdom, Jason loses a sandal. Pelias is afraid when he sees Jason approach, as an oracle has told him that he will be overthrown by a stranger wearing only one sandal. The wicked Pelias pretends to acquiesce but says that the gods have told him that the Golden Fleece must be retrieved for the kingdom first. This is a lie—Pelias assumes that anyone sent on that dangerous journey will never come back. Jason, intrigued by the challenge, assembles a remarkable group of heroes to help him, including Hercules, Theseus, Peleus, and Orpheus. Their ship is named the *Argo,* so the group is called the Argonauts.

The Argonauts face many challenges on the way to Colchis. They first meet the fierce women of Lemnos, who have killed their men, but find them atypically kind. Hercules leaves the crew, and the Argonauts meet an oracle, Phineus. The sons of Boreas, the North Wind, help Phineus by driving off some terrible Harpies who foul his food whenever he tries to eat. Phineus gives the Argonauts information that helps them pass safely through their next challenge—the Symplegades, gigantic rocks that smash together when a ship sail through them. After narrowly avoiding conflict with the Amazons, bloody women warriors, and passing by the chained Prometheus, the Argonauts finally arrive at Colchis.

Though more trials await here, Hera and Aphrodite help Jason. Like Pelias, Aetes pretends to want to give Jason the Fleece but first demands that he complete two tasks that are designed to kill him. Aphrodite sends Cupid to make Aetes's daughter, a witch named Medea, fall in love with Jason and help him through the tasks. The first challenge is to yoke two fierce magical bulls with hooves of bronze and breath of fire, and Medea gives Jason an ointment that makes him invincible. The second task is to use the bulls to plow a field and sow it with dragon's teeth, which causes armed men to spring up from the earth and attack Jason. Medea tells him that if he throws a rock in the middle of the armed men, they will attack each other, not him. After Jason's success, Aetes plots to kill the Argonauts at night, but Medea again intercedes, warning Jason and enabling him to steal the Fleece by putting its guardian serpent to sleep. Medea joins the Argonauts and flees back to Greece. On the way home, she commits the ultimate act of love for Jason: to help evade the ship's pursuers, she kills her own brother, Apsyrtus.

On the way home, the Argonauts pass more challenges, including safely navigating Scylla, the dreaded rock; Charybdis, the whirlpool; and Talus, the giant bronze man. Upon returning, Jason finds that Pelias has killed his father and that his mother has died of sadness. Jason and Medea plot revenge—Medea convinces Pelias's daughters that they will restore Pelias to youth if they kill him, chop him up, and put the pieces into her magic pot. Out of love for their father, they slice him to bits, but Medea leaves the city, taking her magic pot with her after first restoring Jason's father to life.

Medea and Jason have two children, but Jason leaves out of personal ambition to marry the daughter of the king of Corinth, who banishes Medea and her children. Infuriated by the unsympathetic Jason, Medea enacts a terrible revenge, sending her two sons with a beautiful magic robe as a gift for Jason's new bride. When the girl dons the robe, it bursts into flame, consuming her and the king as he rushes to her. Medea then kills the two sons she had with Jason and flies away on a magic chariot. This tragic final chapter in the story of Jason and Medea is the subject of Euripides' play, *Medea*.

SUMMARY: CHAPTER IV — FOUR GREAT ADVENTURES

### Phaëthon

> *Here Phaëthon lies, who drove the Sun-god's car.*
> *Greatly he failed, but he had greatly dared.*
> (See QUOTATIONS, p. 77)

Born on earth, Phaëthon learns that his father is the Sun, so he seeks him out. The Sun, joyous at seeing his son, swears by the river Styx—an unbreakable oath—to grant him any wish. Phaëthon asks to fly the Sun's chariot across the sky. Though the Sun foresees the horrible end, his oath binds him to grant the wish. Phaëthon cannot handle the chariot's wild horses, who rage and set the world on fire. To halt the destruction, Jove kills Phaëthon with a thunderbolt. The magical invisible Eridanus River puts out the flames.

### Pegasus and Bellerophon

A beautiful and strong youth, Bellerophon wants more than anything to possess the winged horse Pegasus. He sleeps in Athena's temple one night, and upon waking finds a golden bridle that enables him to tame the horse. Bellerophon rejects the infatuated wife of a king named Proetus, who accuses him of wrongdoing and sends him on a quest with the intent to kill him. He kills the Chimera, a monster with a lion's head, goat's body, and serpent's tail; defeats the fierce Solymi warriors and the Amazons; but he finally goes too far by trying to use Pegasus to fly up to Olympus. The wise Pegasus bucks Bellerophon, who spends the rest of his days a lonely wanderer while Pegasus becomes the pride of Zeus's stables.

## *Otus and Ephialtes*
Two Giant brothers—sons of Poseidon—Otus and Ephialtes also exhibit pride in the face of the gods, as they claim superiority to the gods and manage to kidnap Ares. They also try to kidnap Artemis, who outwits them, tricking them into killing each other with spears.

## *Daedalus*
The son of master inventor Daedalus, Icarus is also prideful. The architect of the Labyrinth of Minos in Crete, Daedalus is imprisoned with his son. He builds wings for their escape but warns Icarus not to fly too high, as the sun will melt the wings. Icarus does not listen: he flies high, his wings melt, and he plummets to his death in the sea.

## ANALYSIS: CHAPTERS III–IV
The story of Jason is the first real epic in *Mythology*. It follows a common pattern: a hero sets out on an adventure and must pass a number of perils and complete a number of tasks to achieve his goal. Upon returning, they must unseat a usurper and reclaim the throne. This pattern is almost exactly duplicated in the *Odyssey* and the stories of Aeneas, Theseus, and Hercules.

The bloody and dark story of Jason is somewhat unusual, however, as it gives no clear reason why Jason should be considered a hero. He does nothing remotely heroic in the story, aside from confronting danger without cowardice. The Lemnians unaccountably help the Argonauts, the sons of Boreas drive off the Harpies, and Phineus's advice helps them surpass the Clashing Rocks. Jason does not really do anything in these adventures, and his next challenges—yoking the bulls, plowing, defeating the armed men, stealing the Fleece, escaping, and killing Pelias—are accomplished by the enamoured Medea, not by Jason. Yet Medea comes off as the villain at story's end, while Jason is portrayed as her needless victim.

This portrayal of Jason as heroic and Medea as villainous stems from Greek biases against women and "barbaric" foreign civilizations. Though Jason victimizes Medea, as a foreign woman, she is given no sympathy, and is forever portrayed as an evil witch. Indeed, her acts, though performed out of love and devotion, are so shocking and horrible that she cannot possibly be a heroine. This, as we see later, is the case with other mythical figures, such as Tantalus, whose well-intentioned but gruesome acts are punished by the gods.

Indeed, intention is just as meaningless in regards to fate. The crucial theme of humility before fate and the gods resurfaces repeatedly in these stories. Pelias tries to defy fate, wrongly thinking he can avoid death at the hands of the one-sandaled man by killing him. Likewise, Phaëthon, Bellerophon, Otus, Ephialtes, and Icarus warn against the folly of trying to equal the gods. The image of Icarus is the classic symbol of "one who flew too high." Like the crucial trait of obedience, humility before the gods represents a proper understanding of the order of the universe. Mortals secure their place in the world only by remaining subservient to divine powers.

These chapters also focus on the important virtue of hospitality. The code of hospitality—particularly the idea that once one houses a guest, one cannot harm that guest—might seem foreign to us. Aetes cannot kill Jason outright because he has fed him and housed him: "If these strangers had not eaten at my table I would kill them." The same obligation binds Proteus to Bellerophon. Though this straightforward social code might seem odd to us today, it was, as we see in the myths, an important part of ancient civilization.

## Part Three, Chapters I–II

### Summary: Chapter I — Perseus

Hamilton draws the story of Perseus from the later writers Ovid and Apollodorus, though it was also widely popular among the Greeks. One day, the Oracle at Delphi tells King Acrisius of Argos that the future son of his daughter, Danaë, will kill him. Though Acrisius imprisons Danaë to prevent her from ever getting pregnant, Zeus magically enters the prison. Danaë gives birth to a son, Perseus. Acrisius locks Danaë and Perseus in a chest and casts it to sea.

Danaë and her son eventually wash up at the home of Dictys, a kind fisherman whose brother, Polydectes, is the cruel ruler of the area. Polydectes soon wants to get rid of Perseus and marry Danaë, so he comes up with a plan to kill the young man: he convinces Perseus to go kill Medusa, the horrible Gorgon—an impossible feat for a mortal. The gods favor Perseus, however: he receives a mirrored shield from Athena, a magic sword from Hermes, and information on the location of the nymphs of the North—the only ones who know how to kill the Gorgon—from the Graiae, three supernatural gray sisters with only one eye among them. Perseus craftily steals the eye the Graiae share and refuses to return it until they help him. He eventually reaches the mystical land of the Hyperborean nymphs, who give him winged sandals that allow him to fly, a wallet that expands to hold anything, and a cap that makes its wearer invisible. With these, Hermes' sword, and Athena's mirrored shield—which enables him to avoid looking directly at the Gorgons, which would turns him to stone—he creeps into the Gorgons' cave while they are sleeping. The two gods point out Medusa, the only mortal one. While looking at her in the mirror, Perseus chops off her head and puts it in the magic wallet, then begins to fly home.

Along the way, he comes upon Andromeda, a princess who has been chained to a rock because her mother, Cassiopeia, has offended the gods. A sea serpent is about to eat Andromeda, but Perseus cuts off its head and takes Andromeda as his wife. He returns home to find that Polydectes has driven his mother and Dictys into hiding. Perseus goes to Polydectes' palace where all the evil men of the kingdom are gathered. He marches into the meeting and reveals Medusa's head, turning all the men to stone. He lives happily ever after but only after unwittingly fulfilling the prophecy of the Oracle: while participating in a discus-throwing contest, Perseus accidentally hits and kills a spectator, who is, unbeknownst to him, his grandfather Acrisius.

## Summary: Chapter II — Theseus

Hamilton's account of Theseus, the greatest hero of Athens, again draws upon Apollodorus, but it also stitches together details from other writers, some as early as Sophocles. Theseus is the son of the Athenian king, Aegeus, but he grows up with his mother in the south. Aegeus has left a sword and pair of shoes under a giant rock and says that when Theseus gets strong enough to move the rock, he is to be sent to Athens. Theseus reaches maturity, rolls the rock aside, takes the sword and shoes, and sets out on the journey. The dangerous road to Athens is full of bandits, notably Sciron, Sinis, and Procrustes, who delight in torturing passersby. Theseus kills the bandits in the same methods they have used to kill their own victims.

When Theseus arrives in Athens, the evil Medea senselessly convinces Aegeus, who does not realize the stranger is his son, to kill him. At the last minute, Aegeus sees the sword and recognizes the boy. Medea escapes to Asia. Theseus then saves Athens from its obligation to King Minos of Crete. After a son of Minos was killed while a guest in Aegeus's household, Minos beat the Athenians in a war, and now, as punishment, every nine years the Athenians had to send seven girls and seven boys to meet their doom in the Labyrinth of the Minotaur. Theseus offers himself as a victim, promising his father that if he survives, he will replace his ship's black sail with a white one for the return journey so that Aegeus will be able to tell whether his son is alive.

Like Jason, Theseus wins the heart of the enemy king's daughter, Ariadne, who defies Minos and helps Theseus escape the Labyrinth with a ball of golden thread that he unwinds as he walks so that he can find his way back. Theseus finds the Minotaur asleep, beats it to death, and flees to the ship to sail home. Ariadne flees with him, and on the way home, he abandons her when she goes ashore and a fierce wind blows him out to sea. Ariadne dies, which is perhaps what makes Theseus forget to lower the black sail and raise the white one. When Aegeus sees the black sail approaching, he commits suicide by jumping into the sea then named after him—the Aegean.

Theseus becomes king and makes Athens a democracy. He has several minor adventures while king: he helps the Argives after the War of the Seven against Thebes, when the Thebans refuse to allow the defeated to bury their dead (see Part Five, Chapter II); he helps Oedipus and his daughters (same chapter); and prevents Hercules from killing himself after his insanity (see Part Three, Chapter III). Theseus fights the Amazons twice—once attacking them, once defending their attack on Athens—and marries their queen, Hippolyta (also called Antiope), who bears him his son Hippolytus. He is one of the Argonauts (see Part Two, Chapter III) and a participant in the Calydonian Hunt (see Part Three, Chapter IV). He defeats the Centaurs, vicious half-men half-horse beasts, after they kill the bride of his best friend, Pirithoüs. Theseus helps his friend again, when Pirithoüs foolishly decides to pursue Persephone as his next wife. Hades outwits them, tricking them into his Chair of Forgetfulness, which makes their minds blank and paralyzes them. Hercules rescues Theseus, repaying his debt, but Pirithoüs remains there forever.

Theseus's story becomes tragic. He marries Ariadne's sister, Phaedra, who subsequently falls in love with his son, Hippolytus. Hippolytus rejects Phaedra, who kills herself and leaves a suicide note accusing Hippolytus of rape. Theseus curses and exiles Hippolytus, who soon dies. Artemis reveals the truth to Theseus. He then goes to visit his friend, King Lycomedes, who mysteriously kills him.

## Analysis: Chapters I–II

These two stories reinforce earlier themes about fate and the danger of hubris. When King Acrisius tries to alter fate by locking Danaë up and casting her out to sea, his actions only set the stage for that very fate to be fulfilled. Likewise, when Theseus oddly oversteps his place in trying to help Pirithoüs steal Persephone, he fails for the first time and needs Hercules' rescue. These myths explicate their moral lessons by showing that correct behavior is rewarded but rule-breaking—such as hubris towards the gods—is punished.

As Hamilton points out, Perseus's story almost resembles a fairy-tale, with its magic objects and divine intervention. Hermes and Athena tell Perseus almost precisely what to do. Aside from his wily craftiness with the Graiae, his success is due entirely to his sandals, wallet, cap, and sword. Even his motivation is simple, driven by self-preservation and a desire for a beautiful wife. Once he has won these simple aims, he disappears from our view.

Theseus, on the other hand, has many great achievements, and embodies a more highly developed heroism than Perseus. Right from the start, he seeks challenges and wins by his own hand, lifting the rock his father has placed. Then, in the very act of setting off to find his father, he altruistically chooses to better the path for other travelers by killing the bandits. Theseus promptly volunteers himself as a victim for the Minotaur, out of a sense of kinship with the Athenian youth and a desire to end the unfair tribute in blood. Though Theseus escapes from the Labyrinth with Ariadne's golden thread, he conquers the Minotaur himself. Never one to rest on his laurels, he initiates the institution of democracy, serves as a wise judge in disputes, and comes to the aid of justice when the rulers of Thebes withhold it from the Argives. His constant aim is the impartial and balanced protection of decency and the defenseless, and he faces each new challenge with wisdom, gravity, and bravery.

Theseus's story is enduring and deeply culturally rooted, especially in his native Athens. Perseus's tale, in contrast, is a straightforward adventure of pure good versus pure evil. Theseus's story is more intricate, human, and realistic. Interestingly, few of Theseus's challenges come from pure evil or malice—even the adventure of the Minotaur, which seems a case of simple monstrosity, is more complex and with longer roots. The whole tribute of Athenian flesh to

Minos stems from Aegeus's earlier wronging of Minos—the death of a son entrusted to Aegeus's hospitality. Theseus is, then, caught in a complicated situation that predates him. In this sense, his story resembles the great Greek tragedies, which almost universally portray heroes or heroines who begin trapped in the complicated situations they have inherited, and which force them to make difficult decisions through a process of exhaustive soul-searching.

## Part Three, Chapters III–IV

### Summary: Chapter III — Hercules

Hamilton draws her story of Hercules mostly from later writers but also borrows from Greek tragedians. Hercules, born in Thebes, is the son of Zeus and Alcmene, a mortal whom Zeus deceives by disguising himself as her husband. Hercules' demi-god status allows him many liberties. He can challenge the gods and often win, as when he offends the Oracle at Delphi and quarrels with Apollo. He also helps the gods defeat the giants with his superhuman strength; above all else, he is remembered as the strongest man who ever lived. Only magic can harm him, as he overpowers all else. His unequalled strength makes up for deficiencies in intelligence and patience—he can be impetuous, emotional, and careless, and once threatens to shoot an arrow at the sun because it is too hot. Nonetheless, he has boundless courage and a noble sense of right and wrong.

Hercules' strength is evident from his infancy. One night, two giant snakes attack him and his half-brother, Iphicles, in their nursery, but Hercules strangles them both at once. While still a youth he kills the legendary Thespian lion of the Cithaeron woods, taking its skin as a cloak he always wears thereafter. In his youth he also demonstrates a tragic weakness that haunts him his entire life—he rashly and unthinkingly kills one of his teachers, not knowing his own strength. After conquering the warlike Minyans, he marries the princess Megara. He has three children with her, but then Hera, jealous of Zeus's infidelity with Hercules' mother, uses magic to make Hercules go insane and kill his wife and children. Recovering his sanity and seeing what he has done, he rushes to kill himself, but Theseus convinces him to live. Knowing he must purify himself, Hercules goes to the Oracle at Delphi for advice. She tells him to visit his cousin, Eurystheus of Mycenae, who will devise a penance.

Spurred on by Hera, Eurystheus devises a series of twelve impossibly difficult tasks. The first of these Labors of Hercules is to kill the lion of Nemea, a beast that cannot be harmed by weapons; Hercules chokes it to death. Next, he must kill the Hydra, a monster with nine heads, one of which is immortal. A new head grows whenever one of the other heads is chopped off—a problem Hercules solves by burning the neck-stumps and burying the immortal head. In the third task, Hercules captures the sacred golden-horned stag of Artemis and brings it back alive. The fourth task is to capture a giant boar. The fifth, cleaning the stables of King Augeas in a day. The king has thousands of cattle whose manure has not been cleaned in years, so Hercules redirects two rivers to flow through the stable. Athena helps Hercules with his sixth task, which is to rid the people of Stymphalus of a flock of wild birds that terrorize them.

All the other tasks involve the capture of things extremely resistant to captivity: a beautiful wild bull of Minos; the flesh-eating horses of Diomedes; the girdle of Hippolyta, queen of the Amazons; the cattle of Geryon; a three-bodied monster (it is on the way to fulfill this labor that Hercules balances two giant rocks at Gibraltar and Ceuta, on either side of the strait between Spain and Morocco). The eleventh task is to steal the Golden Apples of the Hesperides, the mysterious daughters of Atlas. Journeying to find Atlas, the only one who knows the Hesperides' location, Hercules stops to free Prometheus from his chains. Atlas offers to tell Hercules only if he holds up the world—normally Atlas's job—while Atlas fetches the Apples for him. Atlas gets the fruit but decides he prefers walking around without the weight of the world on his shoulders. Hercules tricks him into taking the earth back, saying he needs to be relieved for a moment to place a pad on his shoulders. Finally, for the twelfth labor, Hercules has to bring Cerberus, the three-headed dog, up from the underworld. Before leaving Hades, Hercules frees his friend Theseus from the Chair of Forgetfulness.

Hercules undergoes other various adventures after his labors, defeating Antaeus—a wrestler who is invincible as long as he touches the ground—and rescuing King Laomedon's daughter, who is being sacrificed to a sea serpent. Hercules also carelessly kills several others along the way: a boy who accidentally spills water on him and a friend whose father, King Eurytus, insults him. As punishment for this last murder, Zeus sends Hercules to be a slave to Queen Omphale of Lydia, who forces him to dress and work as a woman for a year (though some say three years). Despite his errors, Hercules almost always has a clear sense of right and wrong as well as the need to make things right. On the way to kill the wicked Diomedes (owner of the flesh-eating horses), Hercules gets drunk at the house of his friend, Admetus, not knowing that Admetus' wife has just died. When Hercules learns of his friend's loss, he feels so bad about his inadvertent disrespect that he fights and defeats Pluto (Hades) to bring Admetus's wife back from Hades.

One time, however, Hercules refuses to see the error of his ways, and this leads to his death. Angered that Zeus had punished him for inadvertently killing King Eurytus's son, Hercules kills Eurytus and razes his city. One of his captives is a beautiful girl, Iole. Deianira, Hercules' wife, feels threatened, and recalls some magic she earlier acquired, when Hercules shot a centaur named Nessus who insulted Deianira. As Nessus died, he told Deianira to take some of his blood as a potion to use if her husband ever loved anyone more than her. Deianira secretly rubs some of the potion on Hercules' robe. When he puts the robe on, pain surges through his body. He does not die and must end the agony by killing himself, building a giant funeral pyre where he burns himself to death. Ascending to Olympus, Hercules reconciles with Hera and marries her daughter, Hebe.

## Summary: Chapter IV — Atalanta

Atalanta is the greatest female hero, mostly for her role in the Calydonian Hunt—a great hunt for a vicious wild boar Artemis has sent to terrorize the kingdom of a king who forgot to pay her tribute. A large group of heroes hunts the boar, but it is Atalanta who finally causes its death. She first wounds it, and a warrior named Meleager, who is hopelessly in love with her, delivers the mortal blow. His love for her, however, results in his death. Meleager's two uncles insult Atalanta, so he kills them. In turn, Meleager's mother destroys him by burning the magical log that determines the length of his life.

Atalanta has other adventures, most notably beating Peleus, Achilles's father, in a wrestling match. Some say she is one of the heroes who search for the Golden Fleece, but that is unlikely. In another story she has vowed never to marry but has many suitors. To appease them, she agrees to marry anyone who beats her in a race, as she knows she is unbeatable. However, a young man named Melanion (or Milanion or Hippomenes) defeats her with his wits. He carries several golden apples in the race and drops them along the way. Distracted by their beauty, Atalanta loses and marries him. At some point they both offend Zeus and are turned into lions.

## Analysis: Chapters III–IV

Though Hercules is one of the most famous mythical characters—largely due to his colorful and spectacular exploits—he is far from the ideal Greek hero. He causes much misery and must endure much suffering as a result. On one level, he is a very simple character: strong, brave, good-hearted, and not much else. He is unlike the heroes Odysseus, Theseus, or even Perseus, who display wit and cleverness along with a clear awareness of the places of gods and men; Hercules, however, is stubborn, pig-headed, decidedly non-intellectual, and often directly challenges the gods.

His story, therefore, is one of constant struggle between his noble urges and his weaker impulses. Hamilton notes that the secret to Hercules' heroism lies in "his sorrow for wrongdoing and his willingness to expiate it [by which] he showed greatness of soul." His character is brutishly simple, but his story is compelling because it is about a hero struggling with himself. At every turn in his life, Hercules is his own worst enemy and must suffer to correct his errors. After he murders his family—which Hera induces and is not necessarily his fault—he essentially imposes the Twelve Labors upon himself. As Hamilton notes, his heroism stems from his strong sense of morality and his ability to see when he has done wrong. Hercules' refusal to atone for one of his sins—even after Zeus has punished him for it—leads to his downfall. His death emphasizes that wrongdoing, as well as arrogance against the gods, will be punished.

It might seem odd that the intellectual culture of Athens would revere such a simple-minded brute. Yet Hercules' emotional struggle is complex and tragic, and it is this aspect of his character that the great tragedians explore. Indeed, the most satisfying myths are not simple tales of victories over evil but tales of characters who encounter and confront the good and evil causes and consequences of their actions. Hercules is, on one hand, a superheroic character of vast strength and courage. On the other hand, his story, as an adventure tale motivated by his tragic missteps, is a very human one.

Atalanta may appear in this section on four heroes merely because Hamilton desired gender balance. Though a great heroine, her fame and adventures are no match for Perseus, Theseus, or Hercules. Her presence is nonetheless significant, as it is worth noting that the Greek myths do have a tradition of celebrating the female warrior-huntress. From the goddesses Artemis and Athena to the human Amazons and Atalanta, there are numerous proud, fiercely independent women who are every bit equal to men. Though we tend to locate the prototype of a self-sufficient, empowered woman as a twentieth-century phenomenon, these myths demonstrate its existence at a much earlier date.

## Part Four, Chapters I–II

### Summary: Chapter I — The Trojan War

> *A father's hands*
> *Stained with dark streams flowing*
> *From blood of a girl....*     (See QUOTATIONS, p. 77)

In her portrayal of the Trojan War, Hamilton borrows from Homer's *Iliad,* Apollodorus, Greek tragedies, and Virgil's *Aeneid.* The war has its roots in the wedding of King Peleus and the sea-nymph Thetis. When the gods decide not to invite Eris, she is angered and introduces Discord to the banquet hall in the form of a golden apple inscribed with the words "For the Fairest." The vain goddesses argue over who deserves the apple, and the field is narrowed down to Athena, Hera, and Aphrodite. Paris, the son of King Priam of Troy, is selected to judge. All three try to bribe Paris: Hera offers power, Athena offers success in battle, and Aphrodite offers the most beautiful woman in the world—Paris chooses Aphrodite.

Unfortunately, the most beautiful woman in the world, Helen, is already married to King Menelaus of Sparta. Visiting Menelaus, Paris, with Aphrodite's help, betrays his host's hospitality and kidnaps Helen back to Troy. All the Greek kings have at one time courted Helen, so her mother has made them all swear to always support whomever she might choose. When Helen is abducted, the only men who resist conscription are Odysseus, who does not want to leave his home and family, and Achilles, whose mother knows he is fated to die at Troy and holds him back. In the end, however, they join the rest of the Greeks and sail united against Troy. En route, the fleet angers Artemis, who stops the winds from blowing. To appease her, the chief of the Greeks, Agamemnon, is forced to sacrifice his own daughter, Iphigenia.

The battle goes back and forth for nine years. The Trojans, led by Priam's son, Hector, finally gain an advantage when Agamemnon kidnaps the daughter of the Trojan priest of Apollo. Achilles has warned against this, and he is justified when Apollo's fiery arrows nearly destroy the Greek army. Calchas, a Greek prophet, convinces

Agamemnon to free the girl, but Agamemnon demands a replacement in the form of Achilles' prize female captive, Briseis. Furious, Achilles withdraws his troops from battle. Without Achilles, the Greeks seem doomed. The gods have been evenly split thus far: Aphrodite, Ares, Apollo, and Artemis on the side of the Trojans; Hera, Athena, and Poseidon take the Greek side. But Thetis persuades the hitherto neutral Zeus to help the Trojans. Menelaus defeats Paris in combat, however. Aphrodite saves Paris's life, and the armies agree to a truce. But Hera is bent on war, so she makes a Trojan named Pandarus break the truce. When the battle starts again, the great Greek warrior Diomedes nearly kills the Trojan Aeneas, whom Apollo saves. Diomedes even wounds Ares himself.

The Greeks hold their own until Zeus remembers his promise to Thetis and comes down to the battlefield. The Trojans drive the Greeks back toward their ships. That night, Agamemnon agrees to return Briseis, but when Odysseus goes to ask Achilles to accept the apology, he receives a flat refusal. The next day the Greeks lose again without Achilles and are driven even closer to their ships. But then Hera decides to seduce Zeus and give the Greeks an advantage. While the two divinities are indisposed, the great Greek warrior Ajax nearly kills Hector. Discovering the deception, Zeus angrily commands Poseidon to abandon the Greeks, and the Trojans press forward. As the Greeks near defeat, Achilles's best friend, Patroclus, can restrain himself no longer. He convinces Achilles to lend him his armor, thinking that even if Achilles refuses to fight, he himself can help the Greeks by pretending to be Achilles and thus frightening the Trojans. Leading Achilles' men, the Myrmidons, into battle, Patroclus fights valiantly but is killed by Hector's spear. Achilles grieves terribly and decides to return to battle to avenge this death. Thetis, seeing she can no longer hold her son back, gives him armor made by Hephaestus himself.

The Trojans soon retreat inside their impenetrable walls through the huge Scaean gates. Only Hector remains outside, clad in Achilles' own armor taken from Patroclus's corpse. Hector and Achilles, the two greatest warriors of the Trojan War, finally face one another. When Hector sees that Athena stands by Achilles' side while Apollo has left his own, he runs away from Achilles. They circle around and around the city of Troy until Athena disguises herself as Hector's brother and makes him stop. Achilles catches up with Hector, who realizes the deception. They fight, and Achilles, aided by Athena, kills Hector with his spear. Achilles is still so filled with rage over

Patroclus's death that he drags Hector's body over the ground, mutilating it. He takes it back to the Greek camp and leaves it beside Patroclus's funeral pyre for dogs to devour. Such disrespect for a great warrior greatly displeases the gods, who convince Priam to visit Achilles and retrieve Hector's body. Priam speaks to Achilles, who sees the error of his ways. The *Iliad* ends with Hector's funeral.

SUMMARY: CHAPTER II — THE FALL OF TROY

> *We stand at the same point of pain.*
> *We too are slaves.*
> *Our children are crying, calling to us with tears,*
> *"Mother, I am all alone...."*   (See QUOTATIONS, p. 78)

The war itself does not end with Hector's funeral, and Virgil continues the account. Hector is replaced by Prince Memnon of Ethiopia, a great warrior, and the Trojans have the upper hand for a time. But Achilles soon kills Memnon as well, driving the Trojans back to the Scaean gates. There, however, Paris kills Achilles with Apollo's help: Paris shoots an arrow and the god guides it to Achilles' heel, his one vulnerable spot. (Thetis tried to make the infant Achilles invulnerable by dunking his body in the mystical River Styx but forgot to submerge the heel by which she held him.) The Greeks decide Achilles' divine armor should be given to either Odysseus or Ajax, the two greatest Greek warriors remaining. When Odysseus is chosen, Ajax plots revenge, but Athena makes him go crazy. Ajax massacres some cattle, then comes to his senses and, mortified, kills himself.

The prophet Calchas then tells the Greeks that they must capture the Trojan prophet Helenus in order to win. They do so, and Helenus tells them that Troy can only be defeated by the bow and arrows of Hercules. Hercules gave these weapons to Philoctetes, who set out for Troy with the Greeks, who abandoned him along the way. Odysseus and a few others set out to apologize and get him back. Philoctetes returns and promptly kills Paris. The Greeks learn that the Trojans have a sacred image of Athena, the Palladium, that protects them. Odysseus and Diomedes sneak behind enemy lines and steal it. Yet Troy still has the protection of its gigantic walls, which prevent the Greeks from entering. Finally, Odysseus comes up with a plan to build a giant wooden horse and roll it up to the gates, pretending they have surrendered and gone home. One man, Sinon, stays behind, acting as if he is a traitor to the Greeks. He says that although the Greeks retreated, they left the horse as an offering to Athena. He says the Greeks assumed the Trojans would not take it inside the city because of its size, which would thus offend Athena and bring misfortune on the city. Trojans, feeling like they are getting the last laugh, triumphantly bring the horse into the city.

The horse is hollow, however, and Greek chieftains are hiding inside. At night, they creep out and open the city gates. The Greek army, hiding nearby, sweeps into the city and massacres the Trojans. Achilles' son kills Priam. Of the major Trojans, only Aeneas escapes, his father on his shoulders and his son holding his hand. All the men are killed, the women and children separated and enslaved. In the war's final act, the Greeks take Hector's infant son, Astyanax, from his mother, Andromache, and throw him off the high Trojan walls. With this death, the legacy of Hector and Troy itself are finished.

## Analysis: Chapters I–II

The Trojan War is the most famous of all Greek conflicts, and the *Iliad* perhaps the most famous literary work from ancient Greece. As we might expect, this story touches on all the major themes of the myths: hospitality, love, obedience to the gods and to the moral code, and the immutability of fate. The importance of hospitality is evident in Paris's weakness and wickedness in abusing Menelaus's hospitality. The importance of the patriotic moral code is stressed by the catastrophic rift between Agamemnon and Achilles. Likewise, the power of love is shown in its ability to heal Achilles' grief over Patroclus. Morality and obedience to the gods are present throughout, from Agamemnon's sacrifice of Iphigenia to Achilles' return of Hector's body. As in the other myths, the gods reward obedience and goodness and punish disobedience and wickedness. In the war, even the gods bow before fate, as Thetis accepts Achilles' inevitable death and Zeus accepts the inevitable Greek victory.

Above all, the epic of the Trojan War depicts the dark complexity of Greek mythology. The strength of so many of the myths is their depth of character and complex morality. They are not simple fairy tales of good battling evil; they show conflicted characters, ambiguity, and the harshness of the world. Clear villains are conspicuously absent in the *Iliad*: there is no wicked king to provide a foil for a good, shining one. Achilles and Hector, the two main adversaries in the war, are *both* shown to be heroic. Thus, rather than having a standard protagonist-antagonist conflict, the *Iliad* dwells on the brutality and senseless death of war, the cruelty that abounds in the world, and the struggles the heroes have with themselves. Hector is heroic because he remorsefully refuses to stay with his family and instead chooses to face the battle he knows is his destiny.

Worse, the divine sphere provides no relief from the hopelessly bloody and cruel universe depicted in the *Iliad*. Though the gods do uphold a standard of morality, they are not omnipotent, beneficent, or kind. They fight among each other, trick and deceive each other, and reveal themselves as cowardly; even the normally irreproachable Artemis demands a horrific human sacrifice. Thus, the gods represent a higher standard of justice and honor, as when they refuse to allow Hector's body to remain unburied, yet show the same bloodthirstiness and blind bias as the warriors on the battlefield.

As the pain and suffering in the world of the *Iliad* does not follow a clear dichotomy between good and evil, the source of conflict is complex and personal. The heroes struggle with hardships they find all around them, as well as—in Ajax's case—the evil they find within themselves. In this regard, it is interesting that the key turning point of the story is Achilles' return to battle. This is a moment of profound introspection for Achilles, who suffers the death of a best friend he could have saved. Achilles sees that Patroclus has died because he rushed to help his countrymen—something that Achilles, out of wounded pride, would not do. The main struggle Achilles faces, then, is not against a villainous foe but against his own shortcomings and their consequences. Unlike fairy tales that inevitably end with the death of the antagonist and the triumph of the hero, the *Iliad* ends with death of the Trojan hero Hector, a celebration of Hector's courage, and a sober final statement on the tragedy and conflict at the heart of human existence.

## Part Four, Chapter III— The Adventures of Odysseus

### Summary

The following story comes entirely from Homer's other great epic, the *Odyssey*. Though Athena and Poseidon helped the Greeks during the Trojan War, a Greek warrior violates Cassandra in Athena's temple during the sack of Troy, so Athena turns against the Greeks and convinces Poseidon to do the same. The Greeks are beset by terrible storms on the way home; many ships are destroyed and the fleet is scattered. Odysseus and his crew are blown off course, which starts a decade-long series of adventures for the great Greek chief.

The war and his troubles at sea keep Odysseus away from his home, Ithaca, for twenty years. In his absence, his son, Telemachus, has grown into a man, and his wife, Penelope, is besieged by suitors who assume Odysseus is dead. Penelope remains faithful to Odysseus, but the suitors feast at her house all day and live off her supplies. She holds them off by promising to marry after she finishes weaving a shroud for Laertes, Odysseus's father. Every night she secretly undoes the day's work, leaving the job perpetually unfinished. One day, near the end of Odysseus's voyage, the suitors discover Penelope's ruse and become more dangerously insistent.

Athena's anger subsides and her old affection for Odysseus renews, so she decides to set things right. While Poseidon, still angry with Odysseus, is away from Olympus, she convinces the other gods to help Odysseus return home. In disguise in Ithaca, she convinces Telemachus to search for his father. Telemachus goes to Pylos, the home of Nestor, who sends him to Menelaus in Sparta. Menelaus says he has captured Proteus, the shape-shifting sea god, who says Odysseus is being held prisoner of love by the sea nymph Calypso.

At that moment, Hermes is visiting Calypso and relaying Zeus's command that Odysseus be allowed home. Odysseus sets sail on a makeshift raft and is in sight of land when Poseidon catches sight of him, unleashing a storm that again wrecks the homesick Greek. The kind goddess Ino sweeps down and gives him her veil, protecting him from harm in the water. After two days of swimming, Odysseus reaches the land of the Phaeacians and their kind king, Alcinoüs. The king's daughter, Nausicaä, finds Odysseus, naked and filthy from sleeping on the ground, and leads him to the king. Received warmly, Odysseus tells the story of his wanderings.

He and his crew first encountered the Lotus-Eaters, who eat the narcotic lotus flower and live in stupefied bliss. A few men try the drug and do not want to leave, but Odysseus drags them back to the ship. They sail on and dock in front of an inviting cave, where they search for food. There is wine, food, and pens full of sheep in the cave, but the cave's owner, the giant Cyclops Polyphemus, returns. He seals the entrance with a giant boulder, spots the intruders, and eats two of Odysseus's men. He keeps the others trapped in the cave and eats two more at each meal. Odysseus plans an escape, giving Polyphemus wine until he passes out drunk. The men then take a giant red-hot sharpened stake they have made and poke out the monster's only eye. Blinded, Polyphemus cannot find the men and finally rolls back the boulder blocking the entrance and puts his arms in front of it, figuring he will catch the men as they try to run outside. Odysseus has already thought of this, so the Greeks go to the pens and each tie three rams together. The next day the Greeks hang onto the undersides of the sheep as they go out to pasture. As they pass the entrance, Polyphemus feels only the sheep's backs to make sure there are no Greeks riding them, enabling them to escape.

Next, Aeolus, the keeper of the Winds, gives Odysseus a priceless gift, a leather sack that holds all the storm winds. Odysseus can sail home safely as long as he keeps the bag closed, but his inquisitive crew opens the bag, unleashing a fierce storm that blows them to the land of the Laestrygons, cannibals who destroy every ship in the fleet except one. At their next stop, several men scout ahead and encounter the sorceress Circe, who turns them all into pigs except one man lucky enough to escape. Warned, Odysseus sets out for Circe's house armed with an herb Hermes has given him. When Circe cannot affect him with her magic, she falls in love with him. She returns his crew to human form and they live in luxury at her house for a year. She then uses her magic to tell them how to get home: they must travel to Hades and speak to the dead prophet Teiresias. In the world of the dead, Odysseus and his men lure Teiresias's spirit with blood—a favorite drink of the dead—and ask his help. He says that Odysseus will eventually reach home. He advises them not to harm the oxen belonging to the Sun, as terrible things would happen. Before departing Hades, the Greeks talk with some of their old war comrades, including Achilles and Ajax.

Circe has also given them another piece of information—that they must not listen to the Sirens, women who lure men to death with singing that makes them forget everything. Passing the island of the Sirens, the crew plugs their ears with wax, but the insatiably curious Odysseus requests to be tied to the mast with his ears left open. The ship then passes between Scylla and Charybdis, the dreaded rock-and-whirlpool duo that destroys many ships. They finally arrive at the island of the Sun, where the famished men recklessly slaughter and eat one of the oxen while Odysseus is away. The Sun destroys their ship, drowning everyone but Odysseus. He is carried to the island of Calypso, where he is held for many years.

After hearing this long account, the kind Phaeacians have pity on Odysseus and quickly prepare a ship to take him home. He falls asleep on board and awakens on a beach in Ithaca. Athena comes to him, tells him he is home, and begins to craft a way for him to reclaim his wife and home with a surprise entrance. She transforms him into an old beggar and sends him to stay with Eumaeus, his faithful swineherd. Athena then goes to Telemachus and tells him to return home but to stop by the swineherd's shack on the way. There, Athena transforms Odysseus back to his normal form. The father and son are reunited and come up with a plan to get rid of the suitors. Odysseus again disguises himself as a beggar and goes to his palace. Only Argos, his old dog, recognizes him. Argos dies when Odysseus, trying to preserve his disguise, ignores the dog.

Inside, the boorish suitors mock the beggar and one even hits him. Offended by this breach of hospitality, Penelope orders the old nurse of the house, Eurycleia, to attend to the stranger. As the old woman washes him, she notices a scar on his foot. As she has served the house for many years, she recognizes the scar and the beggar as Odysseus. He makes her promise not to tell a soul, even his wife. The next day, Penelope decides to hold a contest: whoever can string Odysseus's gigantic bow and shoot an arrow through twelve rings can marry her. All the suitors try and fail, but then the beggar stands up and asks for a try. The suitors scoff, but the beggar quickly and easily strings the massive bow and shoots an arrow with dead aim. He then turns and begins shooting the suitors. Taken off guard, they reach for their weapons, but Telemachus has hidden them all. They try to run away, but Telemachus and Eumaeus, to whom Odysseus revealed himself earlier that morning, have locked all the doors. Soon all the suitors, even a priest, have been killed—only a bard is spared, as Odysseus remembers how much the gods favor song and poetry. Odysseus finally reveals himself to Penelope, and after twenty years of separation, they live happily ever after.

---

## ANALYSIS

If the *Iliad* has given Western culture a model of heroic warfare, with mores of bravery, strength, and honor, the *Odyssey* has provided something else entirely. It is not an epic not of social and political communities and relationships, but an epic portrayal of one man over the course of many years. As such, it is a closer ancestor to artistic forms more familiar to us, such as the novel or film. Even the word *odyssey* itself has entered the language, meaning a long wandering, voyage, or quest. While the *Iliad* is often characterized in terms of its grandeur and stately glory, the *Odyssey*, a far more seductive tale, has drawn readers by virtue of its sheer, engaging delight.

Odysseus has fascinated generations of writers, from Dante to James Joyce. He is perhaps the most complex and, in a way, *modern* character of all of Greek literature. His motivations are many, which makes us relate to him and believe his experience of emotion. It is not as easy to relate to Achilles, half-divine and invulnerable aside from his heel, or Agamemnon, willing to sacrifice his daughter based on a prophet's advice and a vow he has made. Odysseus is more human and practical-minded, relying on his own sharp wits rather than trusting himself to divine aid, as other characters do.

As we are able to understand where Odysseus is coming from, we can also spot those actions of his that have less than virtuous motives. A prime example is his stay with Circe: basking in luxury with a beautiful mistress, he whiles away an entire year feasting and drinking, unfaithful to a wife and son who, at great danger and in much unhappiness, are trying to hold his house together. Likewise, Odysseus wishes to hear the Sirens' song out of curiosity but also out of a desire for pleasure; to attain this wish, he is willing to abandon prudence and to put himself above his fellow sailors. This aspect of Odysseus has led some of the epic's interpreters to see him as thirsty for experience, regardless of the cost to himself or to those, like Penelope and Telemachus, to whom he owes allegiance.

At its heart, the *Odyssey* is about the importance of memory—of one's past and one's true role. Forgetfulness recurs as an ever-tempting evil. It is easy to taste the lotus blossoms to feel happy and wish to stay forever, to sit feet of the singing Sirens, and to stay in beauty and luxury with Circe. These specific instances are symbolic echoes of the temptation of forgetfulness that permeates the entire epic. We may even wonder how Odysseus, after ten years of the despair and triumphant ecstasy of war, can go back to his old married life. This challenge resonates just as powerfully today, rooted not in a particular time or culture but in the human condition itself.

## Part Four, Chapter IV — The Adventures of Aeneas

### Summary

> *[The Roman race was] destined to bring under [its] empire the peoples of earth, to impose the rule of submissive nonresistance, to spare the humbled and to crush the proud.* (See QUOTATIONS, p. 80)

NOTE: Because this story was taken from Latin sources, Roman names are used.

Written during the Pax Augusta, a time of great optimism for Rome, Virgil's *Aeneid* chronicles the adventures of Aeneas, the Trojan hero and mythical progenitor of the Roman people. Due to the help of his mother, he is the lone Trojan able to escape defeat at the hands of the Greeks, fleeing with his father on his back and his son in his hand. Aeneas eventually winds up in Italy, where his son founds the city Alba Longa, the predecessor of Rome. Between the two cities, however, Aeneas has a long journey and many adventures.

In a dream, Aeneas is told that he is destined to sail to Italy, known then as Hesperia, the Western Country. On the way, he and his crew encounter the same Harpies whom the Argonauts battled. Unable to defeat them, they are forced to escape. They next encounter Hector's widow, Andromache, enslaved by Achilles' son after the war. After her captor's death, she marries the Trojan prophet Helenus. Helenus tells Aeneas that he should land on the western coast of Italy and gives him directions and tells him how to avoid the dire Scylla and Charybdis. He seemingly does not know about other dangers along the route. Luckily, when the Trojans land on the island of the Cyclopes, they meet a sailor whom Ulysses (Odysseus) has left behind. They escape just as Polyphemus charges the ship.

Juno is still angry with the Trojans, however, as she still resents Paris choosing Venus over her and has learned that Aeneas's descendants are fated to found a city that will one day destroy Carthage, her favorite city. Juno recruits Aeolus, King of the Winds, to send a gigantic storm. Though Neptune's intervention saves the Trojans, they are blown off course all the way to Africa, near Carthage, of all cities. Juno conspires to have Aeneas fall in love with Carthage's queen, Dido, figuring that if he does, he will not leave Carthage. Venus makes her own plan, however, and sends Cupid to ensure that Dido falls in love with Aeneas and that Aeneas never reciprocates the feelings. Nonetheless, as Dido lavishes attention on Aeneas and his men, he grows used to the luxury and lingers in Carthage. At last, Jupiter, acting on Venus's behalf, sends Mercury to Aeneas. Mercury urges Aeneas to go fulfill his destiny, so he soberly takes his leave of a sobbing Dido. Sailing away, he sees smoke rising from Carthage, never knowing that the source is her funeral pyre.

Helenus had also told Aeneas to find the prophetic Sibyl of Cumae upon reaching Italy. They find the Sibyl, who says she must take Aeneas to the underworld to meet his father, Anchises, who has died earlier in the journey. To travel to the underworld, Aeneas and his friend Achates must find a mystical golden bough that gains them admittance. Venus eventually leads them to the bough, which Aeneas bears as he and the Sibyl enter the underworld. They pass by many horrors—lost souls, frightening spirits of Disease and Hunger, even Dido herself, who refuses to acknowledge Aeneas. Charon sees the golden bough and ferries them across his river. They mollify Cerberus with cake and finally find Anchises, who shows Aeneas the souls who will one day rise to be his future descendants. He also tells Aeneas where and how to establish his new home in Italy.

Aeneas returns to the surface and sails up the Italian coast with his crew. Latinus, king of the Latins, warmly receives them. Latinus plans to marry his daughter, Lavinia, to the majestic Aeneas. Juno, however, makes Alecto, one of the Furies, cause trouble. Alecto convinces Latinus's wife to oppose the marriage, and Alecto tells Turnus, King of the Rutulians and suitor of Lavinia, about Aeneas. Finally, Alecto makes Ascanius, Aeneas's son, unwittingly kill a certain stag very popular among the Latins. The advancing army of the Rutulians joins with the Latins to oppose the small band of Trojans. The two armies are also aided by Mezentius, a cruel ex-leader of the Etruscans, and Camilla, a renowned female warrior. Aeneas again receives divine help, however. Father Tiber, god of the famous Roman river, tells him to retreat upstream to find Evander, king of the town that will one day become Rome. There, Evander and his son, Pallas, receive Aeneas warmly but can offer no real help. Evander tells Aeneas that he can seek the help of the powerful Etruscans, who are anxious to get revenge against the tyrannical Mezentius. Evander gives the few men, including Pallas, whom he can spare.

While Aeneas seeks these allies, the Trojans face a huge offensive from Turnus. They must get word to Aeneas, but Nisus and Euryalus are the only Trojans brave enough to sneak past enemy lines to send the message. Euryalus is captured and, Nisus, rather than run away, tries to save Euryalus, only to be killed alongside him. Aeneas returns with Etruscan reinforcements. After the deaths of Camilla, Pallas, and others, Turnus and Aeneas meet in single combat. Aeneas kills Turnus, marries Lavinia, and founds the Roman people.

## Analysis

This is the only chapter exclusively devoted to a distinctly Roman—not Greek—myth. The story is taken from Virgil's *Aeneid* and displays the similarities and differences between this epic and the other myths. The numerous similarities show the compatibility of the Greek and Roman worldviews. Most of these myths moved easily from one culture to the other. The form of the *Aeneid* is similar to the epics of Odysseus, Jason, and Perseus—and, to a lesser degree, Hercules and Theseus. A hero sets out in search of glory but, by the will of the gods, travels a long journey full of perilous adventures. At the end of the journey, he encounters a violent king whom he eventually defeats. Though he is challenged throughout by a god who is bent on his destruction, in the end he achieves his destiny.

The role of fate is strong in the *Aeneid:* Aeneas is destined to found the Roman race, and nothing, not even Juno, can stand in his way. The goddess is helpless before fate, and despite her best intentions, she cannot save Carthage. The idea of myth-as-fable also returns here, as the *Aeneid* is also a fable of the origins of Rome and a political fable on Rome's gripping defeat of arch-rival Carthage.

The most interesting similarity between the *Aeneid* and the Greek myths are their complex view of good and evil. Evil is not concentrated in a single demonic antagonist; Aeneas faces challenges that rise from himself and out of the web of circumstances—many of them beyond his control—in which he finds himself. In this regard, Aeneas's affair with Dido is interesting: despite the luxury of his stay in Carthage, the gods pluck him out and send him back into the fray so that he may achieve his destiny for the benefit of future generations. It may seem cruel that Dido kills herself strictly because she is caught between the warring desires of gods—Juno, Venus, and Zeus—who all have their own priorities. However, the needless suffering the gods cause is an essential part of the worldview that uses myths to attempt to explain the problem of inexplicable evil.

Though the *Aeneid* resembles Greek epics in some respects, in other ways it is foreign. We see this in the nature of Aeneas's heroism. Most of the Greek heroes display intelligence, wit, depth, and greatness of soul, and mortal fallibility that causes introspective struggle and growth. As Hamilton points out, Roman society placed far more emphasis on pure military courage and strength. She quotes from Virgil: "[The Romans] left to other nations such things as art and science, and ever remembered that they were destined to bring under their empire the peoples of earth . . . to spare the humbled and crush the proud." Aeneas—a brave warrior who sacrifices love for duty—fits this mold. The final episode of the *Aeneid,* in which Aeneas becomes a figure of godlike power, is non-Greek. Rather, it typifies the militaristic and grandiose outlook of the Romans—rulers of the largest empire in history at the time of Virgil's writing.

# Part Five, Chapters I–II

## Summary: Chapter I — The House of Atreus

The dynastic dramas of the House of Atreus and the Royal House of Thebes are taken from the works the Greek tragedians Euripides, Aeschylus, and Sophocles. Euripides wrote of the House of Atreus, which includes Atreus's son, Agamemnon, his family (Clytemnestra, Iphigenia, Orestes, and Electra), and his brother, Menelaus. The family is cursed because an ancestor, Tantalus, a son of Zeus who often visited Olympus, mysteriously decided to kill, cook, and serve his son Pelops to the Olympians. Discerning his heinous crime, the gods send Tantalus to be tormented in Hades, where he stands in a pool of water with fruit dangling above his head. The water sinks away when he bends to drink it, and the fruit rises up when he reaches to eat it. He is eternally *tantalized*—a term we use today.

Tantalus's crime initiates generations of violence and tragedy, each crime begetting further bloodshed. Pelops, restored to life by the gods, seeks to marry the princess Hippodamia. She can only be won by the suitor who beats her father in a chariot race; if the suitor loses, he is killed. In one version, Hippodamia and her father's charioteer, Myrtilus, conspire to give Pelops the victory, but Pelops later kills Myrtilus, bringing further bad luck on his family. Tantalus's daughter Niobe decides she is the equal of the gods and demands that the people of Thebes worship her. As punishment, Apollo and Artemis kill her seven sons and seven daughters. Weeping continually, she turns into a rock always wet with tears. Next, Pelops's son Thyestes seduces the wife of his brother, Atreus, who then kills Thyestes's two children and serves them to their father for dinner.

In the newest generation, Agamemnon, Menelaus's brother, sacrifices his daughter Iphigenia to placate Artemis and procure favorable sailing winds during the Trojan War. Agamemnon's wife, Clytemnestra, takes a lover—Aegisthus, son of Thyestes—while Agamemnon is away in Troy. Outraged at the sacrifice of her daughter Iphigenia, she plots revenge against her husband, while Aegisthus vows revenge for his father. When Agamemnon returns from Troy with Cassandra, the prophetess everyone always ignores, Cassandra foretells her and Agamemnon's deaths but is unheeded. The two enter the palace, and Clytemnestra and Aegisthus kill them.

Two of Agamemnon's children still live to perpetuate the bloodshed: his daughter, Electra, whom Aegisthus and Clytemnestra treat cruelly, and son, Orestes, whom a family friend has taken to protect him from Aegisthus. Orestes sets out for vengeance when he comes of age—even though he knows this means the terrible crime of matricide—and the Oracle at Delphi confirms him in this path. Returning to Mycenae, he runs into Electra, who is overjoyed and eager for him to avenge their father. Pretending to be a messenger bearing news of Orestes' death, Orestes is welcomed into the palace, where he kills his mother and her lover. He instantly sees the terrible avenging Furies pursuing him, and he begins years of frenzied wanderings. Finally, with Apollo's aid, he appeals to Athena, who pities him and turns the Furies into the Eumenides, "protectors of the suppliant." The curse of the House of Atreus finally ends.

In another version of the story, Artemis grows horrified just before Iphigenia's sacrifice and rescues her. Artemis brings Iphigenia to the land of the Taurians and makes her a priestess of her own temple. Regrettably, this job involves sacrificing humans, so Iphigenia goes about her duties very reluctantly. In this version, Athena has not completely absolved Orestes of guilt. The Oracle at Delphi tells Orestes that for his last cleansing act he must go to the land of the Taurians and procure the image of Artemis from its temple. Orestes and his friend Pylades set out on the quest, but the Taurians capture them almost immediately and intend to sacrifice them.

Orestes is taken to Iphigenia, the priestess, but the siblings fail to recognize each other because they have been separated for so long. Preparing Orestes and Pylades for death, Iphigenia asks where they are from. On hearing they are from Mycenae, she asks them about her family. She offers to set Pylades free if he takes a message to her brother, Orestes, telling him that she is alive and that he must rescue her. Orestes jumps up and reveals his identity. The three begin their escape with the image of Artemis. King Thoas of the Taurians pursues, but lets them escape when Athena says they are fated to do so.

SUMMARY: CHAPTER II — THE ROYAL HOUSE OF THEBES

> *"What creature," the Sphinx asked him, "goes on four feet in the morning, on two at noonday, on three in the evening?"*    *(See* QUOTATIONS, *p. 79)*

Unlike the House of Atreus, the House of Thebes is named after a city, not a person. The dynastic head, Cadmus, is a brother of Europa, the woman Zeus kidnaps while she is a cow. After her kidnapping, her father sends her brothers to look for her. The Oracle at Delphi tells Cadmus to break off from the group and establish his own city. Fortune blesses his endeavor, but his children are not so lucky. He has four daughters, all of whom experience tragedy: Semele dies while pregnant with Dionysus; Ino becomes the wicked stepmother of Phrixus (from the story of the Golden Fleece) and commits suicide after her husband kills their son; Agave is driven mad by Dionysus and kills her own son, Pentheus; Autonoë's son, Actaeon, accidentally sees the naked Artemis, who kills him. In the end, the gods turn Cadmus and his wife, Harmonia, into serpents for no reason.

The family's greatest misfortune, however, descends upon Cadmus's great-great-grandson, Oedipus. The Oracle at Delphi tells Oedipus's father, King Laius of Thebes, that a son of his will one day kill him and marry his wife. When Oedipus is born, Laius leaves the child tied up on a mountain to die. Years later, Laius is killed by a man he meets on a highway, who everyone believes is a stranger.

In Laius's absence, Thebes is besieged by the Sphinx, a monster who devours anyone who cannot answer her riddle. One day, Oedipus, who has grown up in Corinth as the son of King Polybus, approaches. He has left home because the Oracle at Delphi told him he would one day kill his father. Like Laius, he too wants to subvert fate. The Sphinx asks, "What creature goes on four feet in the morning, two in the afternoon, and three in the evening?" Oedipus gives the correct answer, "Man"—a man crawls as a baby, walks on two legs as an adult, and needs a cane when elderly. The Sphinx, outraged, kills herself. As his reward for freeing the city, Oedipus becomes king and marries the widowed queen, Jocasta.

A terrible plague visits Thebes. Oedipus sends Jocasta's brother, Creon, to the Oracle at Delphi to ask the gods how to fix the situation. Creon returns to say that the plague will lift once Laius's murderer is punished. Oedipus searches for the murderer, eventually consulting the seer Teiresias for help. Teiresias uses his powers to see what has happened, but does not want to tell Oedipus the horrible truth. Oedipus forces him, and the old man says that Oedipus himself is the guilty party. Oedipus and Jocasta piece events together: on the road from Delphi, Oedipus killed a man in a heated argument; they now realize that man was Laius. A messenger from Polybus enters and Oedipus learns that he is not Polybus's true son. He realizes that he is Laius's son and has fulfilled the horrible prophecy. Horrified, Jocasta kills herself and Oedipus gouges out his own eyes.

Oedipus abdicates the throne but remains in Thebes, and the throne passes to Creon. Oedipus is suddenly exiled and has only Antigone, his daughter, by his side to guide him. He finally rests in Colonus, a place near Athens sacred to the Eumenides. In the end, the kindly Theseus honors Oedipus for his unwitting suffering, and the tortured old man dies in peace. Meanwhile, his other daughter, Ismene, has remained in Thebes, and his two sons, Eteocles and Polyneices, fight over the throne. Eteocles eventually wins, but Polyneices assembles an army to attack the city. He convinces six other chieftains to join him, and the seven attack the seven gates of Thebes.

Teiresias tells Creon that Thebes will be saved if Creon's son, Menoeceus, dies. Creon tries to protect the boy from battle, but the impetuous youth, believing he must make this sacrifice, rushes out to his death. Thebes is ultimately victorious, but Eteocles and Polyneices kill each other. Polyneices' dying words express his wish to be buried in his home city, but Creon decrees that anyone who buries any of the six dead enemy leaders—including Polyneices—will be put to death. Antigone, now back in Thebes, is horrified and defies the law, burying her brother. True to his word, Creon executes her.

Though Polyneices is buried, five of the six dead chieftains still lie unburied. Adrastus, the only survivor of the seven, petitions Theseus for help. When negotiations fail, Theseus marches against Thebes, defeats them, forces them to honorably bury the dead, and then nobly retreats, having served justice. The sons of the dead men are not satisfied, however, and eventually band together in a group known as the Epigoni (the "after-born") and level Thebes. In the end, all that is left of the city is a necklace Hephaestus gave to Harmonia upon her wedding to Cadmus.

## Analysis: Chapters I–II

The two most famous stories here are that of Orestes—taken from Aeschylus's *Oresteia*, of which *Agamemnon* is the first play—and Oedipus, taken from Sophocles' *Oedipus* trilogy. Both works concern the central idea that no deed goes without consequence, but the two myths deal with that idea in different ways. Oedipus unwittingly commits a crime, even when he does everything in his power to avoid doing so, because destiny has decreed it. Orestes, on the other hand, consciously chooses to punish evil and thereby commits an evil act himself. Both stories' moral dilemmas are complex.

On the simplest level, both myths concern bad things that happen to good people. Oedipus is, overall, a good man. He does kill his father on the highway, but it is implied that it is done in self-defense. Oedipus acts heroically: he bravely faces the Sphinx, frees Thebes, rules fairly, and fervently searches for Laius's killer. When he learns the evils he has committed, he punishes himself harshly and commits himself to a life of contemplation. Oedipus's heroism comes not from great adventures but from coping with the impossibly cruel hand fate has dealt him. He withstands the worst the world has to offer with a stoic endurance. In the end, he is rewarded for his heroism, dying a peaceful death under the eye of Theseus.

Despite his heroism, Oedipus spends the bulk of his life in horrible suffering. He is simply a victim of cruel destiny. Again, evil abounds in the world of Greek myths, and many stories focus on characters who struggle with this inevitable wickedness of the world around them. Oedipus's story, above all, highlights the immutability of fate, no matter how cruel. Both Laius and Oedipus are told of the pain that lurks in their future, and both set out to change their fate. By doing so, they inadvertently set in motion a chain of events that fulfills their fate. In the world of Oedipus, evil is an inevitability that no one, no matter how virtuous, can escape.

Orestes, however, has more agency, more ability to choose his path. Unlike Oedipus, whose actions are largely blind, Orestes takes vengeance upon his mother by his own choosing. The intricacy of Aeschylus's *Oresteia* lies in the choice Orestes must make: it is not a simple selection between good and evil but a choice of whether to accept the will of the gods or ignore it, to accept his family legacy and fate or throw them off. Orestes feels compelled to accept his destiny, but it is important to note that he could have walked away.

The moral world of the *Oresteia* is, nonetheless, almost as cruel as the world of *Oedipus*. It is the gods who set the violent chain of events in motion, beginning with Artemis's demand for Iphigenia's sacrifice. When Orestes is faced with a choice, he knows the gods demand an act of vengeance for Agamemnon's murder, even though he also knows he is also forbidden to slay his mother. He is in a lose-lose situation and is therefore heroic in his brave choice of a path that he knows will cause him pain. In the end, his heroism is rewarded when the Furies turn into the Eumenides. The moment almost recalls Christian imagery, as Orestes chooses a path of suffering and the entire world is purified as a result.

Both stories offer bleak visions of justice in the world. Unlike the simpler Greek myths—such as the stories of Tantalus and Creon—in which good is rewarded and evil is punished, these stories involve essentially good characters who suffer by little or no fault of their own. Other episodes, such as the Labors of Hercules, the story of the Trojan War, and the trials of Odysseus, have a similar view of the ubiquity of evil. The protagonists of those stories, however, become heroes in their struggle against and, for the most part, triumph over that evil. The stories of Oedipus and Orestes, however, occupy a darker universe than other myths, as both men must accept cruel fates and have no opportunity for epic adventure or glory.

## Part Five, Chapter III; Part Six, Chapters I–II

### Summary: Part Five, Chapter III — The Royal House of Athens

Hamilton takes these stories from Latin poets, largely Ovid, but also borrows from the Greek tragedians, which increases the stories' pathos and reduces their sensationalism and gory detail. The Royal House of Athens is notable in the number and degree of supernatural feats that befall its members. The ancestor is Cecrops, who in some cases is a magical half-man, half-dragon creature. Cecrops is said to have chosen Athena over Poseidon to be the protector of Athens. The angered Poseidon floods the land, and the men of Athens, who have voted for the god, take the vote away from the more numerous women. In other stories, Cecrops is merely the son of Erechtheus, a great Athenian king. Erechtheus has two sisters, Procne and Philomela. Procne is married to Tereus, a son of Ares. When Tereus sees the lovely Philomela, he seduces her into a false marriage by telling her that Procne has died. When Philomela learns the truth, Tereus cuts out her tongue and imprisons her to prevent her from telling anyone. He then tells Procne that Philomela has died. But Philomela weaves a beautiful tapestry as a gift for her sister and secretly embroiders into it the story of her troubles. Procne then rescues her sister and, for revenge, kills Itys—her son with Tereus—and cooks him and serves him to his father. The women escape, but Tereus pursues. As he is about to catch them, the gods take pity on the women and turn them into birds: Procne becomes the beautiful singing nightingale, the tongueless Philomela into the songless swallow.

Erechtheus also has a daughter, Procris, who is married to Cephalus. Just after their wedding, Aurora, the goddess of the dawn, falls in love with Cephalus and kidnaps him. He resists her advances and finally she gives up but not before spitefully planting the suggestion that his wife may not have been faithful as he has. To test it, Cephalus returns home disguised as a stranger and repeatedly tries to seduce Procris, but she always remains faithful to her missing husband. One day, however, she briefly hesitates before rejecting his advances. He becomes angry and reveals his deception, and Procris runs away, furious. Realizing his error, Cephalus follows and apologizes. The two reunite, but tragedy strikes again later when, while hunting, Cephalus accidentally kills Procris with his javelin.

Two of Procris's sisters also have tragic love stories. One, Orithyia, wins the heart of Boreas, the North Wind. Her family opposes the marriage, but Boreas carries the girl off. Creüsa is kidnapped and raped by Apollo. Shamed at the encounter, she bears their baby boy in secret and leaves him to die in the same cave where Apollo assaulted her. Creüsa later feels guilty and goes to retrieve him, but he has vanished. Her father, meanwhile, has married her to a man named Xuthus. Unable to conceive a child, the pair go to the Oracle at Delphi for advice. While Xuthus confers with one of the priests, Creüsa speaks to a beautiful young priest named Ion, wanting to ask, out of Xuthus's earshot, what happened to the baby she abandoned. Xuthus suddenly appears and hugs Ion, saying that Apollo has told him that Ion will become his own son. An older priestess reveals that she found Ion as a baby, wrapped in a cloak and veil. Creüsa recognizes the garments as her own and realizes that Ion is her son. Athena then appears and confirms this revelation, announcing that Ion will one day become a great king of Athens.

## SUMMARY: PART SIX, CHAPTER I — MIDAS — AND OTHERS

### Midas

Midas, a king of Phrygia, performs a favor for Bacchus and is granted one wish in return. Midas foolishly wishes for the power to turn everything he touches into gold. As a result he is unable to eat or drink. Bacchus tells Midas to wash himself in the river Pactolus to remove the spell. Midas later serves as the judge of a music contest between Apollo and Pan. When Midas stupidly calls Pan the better musician, Apollo changes his ears to those of a donkey.

### Aesculapius

Apollo once loved a mortal woman named Coronis who, for a change, cheats on him. He learns of the treachery and kills her but saves her unborn child. He takes the infant boy, Aesculapius, to the centaur Chiron, who raises him and trains him in the arts of medicine. Aesculapius is such a good doctor that he raises a man, Theseus's son Hippolytus, from the dead. Because this is a power no mortal should have, the angry Zeus strikes Aesculapius dead with a thunderbolt. Apollo, enraged at his son's death, attacks the Cyclopes, makers of Zeus's thunderbolts. Zeus condemns Apollo to serve as a slave to King Admetus for a number of years.

### *The Danaïds*

The fifty daughters of Danaüs, the Danaïds are pursued by their fifty male cousins. Danaüs is opposed to the marriages, but the men somehow capture the women and arrange for a gigantic marriage ceremony. Danaüs gives each daughter a dagger. On the wedding night, each girl except one, Hypermnestra, kills her new husband. Danaüs imprisons Hypermnestra for her treachery, but the other girls receive worse torment in the afterlife. They must fill a series of jars with water. The jars are full of holes, so their task never ends.

### *Glaucus and Scylla*

A fisherman who eats magic grass, Glaucus becomes a sea-god. He falls in love with the nymph Scylla, who resists his advances. He asks Circe for a love potion, but she falls in love with him. Circe instead makes a magic poison and pours it into Scylla's bath water. When Scylla touches the water, she becomes the famous rock-monster that later torments the Argonauts, Odysseus, and Aeneas.

### *Erysichthon*

Erysichthon dared to cut down Ceres' (Demeter's) sacred giant oak tree. As punishment, Ceres condemns him to starve to death, no matter how much food he eats. He sells everything he has, including his daughter, for food. His daughter prays to Poseidon to free her from slavery, and the god helps her by transforming her into a fisherman so that her master will not recognize her. She returns to her father, and they perpetrate the scheme again and again: Erysichthon sells her into slavery, and she then transforms and escapes. Erysichthon remains hungry, however, and he finally dies of starvation.

### *Pomona and Vertumnus*

Pomona, a Roman nymph, loves only her fruit orchards. Vertumnus loves her, but she ignores him. One day, he sneaks into her orchard disguised as an old woman, slips up to her, and kisses her. In disguise, he explains that a youth named Vertumnus cares for her and for the same fruit trees she loves. He reminds her that Venus hates women who reject love. He reveals himself as Vertumnus. Pomona relents, and the two cultivate the orchard for the rest of their lives.

### SUMMARY: PART SIX, CHAPTER II
NOTE: As this chapter summarizes what Hamilton categorizes as less important myths, the following is a brief listing and summary of several of the most recognizable characters.

*Arachne*  Minerva's equal at weaving, whom the jealous goddess changes into the ever-weaving spider.

*Callisto*  A girl who attracts Zeus's fancy and whom Hera turns into a bear. Zeus rescues her and makes her into stars.

*Chiron*  The great centaur whom Hercules accidentally kills.

*Epimenedes*  A man who sleeps for fifty-seven years, then later cures Athens of a plague.

*The Hyades*  Six daughters of Atlas who raise Dionysus and, as a reward, are transformed into stars.

*Leto*  Impregnated by Zeus, she mothers Artemis and Apollo.

*Orion*  A great hunter, he becomes a constellation after death.

*The Myrmidons*  Fierce soldiers whom Zeus creates out of ants, they later serve as Achilles' soldiers.

*The Pleiades*  Seven daughters of Atlas whom Orion pursues. Changed into stars, two of them have famous children.

*Sisyphus*  He angers Zeus and is punished in Hades with the task of pushing uphill a rock that eternally rolls back down.

---

### ANALYSIS: CHAPTER III, CHAPTERS I–II
The final Greek and Roman myths are full of minor characters and stories. A few names—Orion, Sisyphus, Arachne—are familiar, but most of these stories are obscure. They do not display much thematic unity but are largely a potpourri of themes we have seen earlier. Indeed, what the pattern that emerges is the simplicity of most of these stories. Unlike the complex heroic epics, many of these are fables or simple tales of good and evil. They fit nicely with the moral and cultural world we have already seen: we again see the power and reward of love, the importance of obedience to the gods, and

the inflexibility of fate. What is striking is the straightforwardness of the stories' moral lessons: the Danaïds kill their husbands and are punished; Coronis is unfaithful to Apollo and is killed. In contrast, the stories of Odysseus or Orestes are full of complexity, ambiguity, and struggle, with difficult moral questions and protagonists with great depth of character. The characters of these simpler myths have survived largely as conceits upon which to overlay artistic creations or as rigid symbols with clear denotations. Hero and Leander, for example, occur in literature as the stereotypical star-crossed lovers, while Arachne represents the arrogance of a human when she makes objects she deems equal to Nature or the work of the gods.

The one well-developed story here—that of Philomela, Procne, and Tereus—is alien to our modern sensibility and even, perhaps, bears the marks of an earlier stage of Greek civilization. Hamilton implies this idea when she notes that Philomela lived so long ago that it was before writing was invented, which is why she was forced to weave her story. Philomela's choice of medium has made her story a rich analogy for issues of representation and self-expression, particularly for women. Scholars and critics have wondered what it might mean to be stripped of one's voice, whether by self, by society, or by trauma. Perhaps the most famous usage of Philomela in this regard is in T. S. Eliot's *The Waste Land*. Broken lines in Eliot's poem, such as the one word "Tereu," enact Philomela's inability to name what has happened to her and her heartbreaking struggle to regain her voice. Eliot uses the metaphor to describe the devastation in Europe after World War I. Despite Philomela's resonance in Western culture, nowhere does she, Procne, or Tereus attain the gravity, depth of character, sense of moral agency, and emotional repercussions we see in Orestes and Oedipus.

## PART SEVEN, INTRODUCTION & CHAPTERS I–II

SUMMARY: INTRODUCTION

The only two original sources of Norse mythology are two Icelandic texts, the *Elder Edda* (first written around A.D. 1300 but containing earlier tales) and the *Younger Edda* (written by Snori Sturluson at the end of the 1100s). The Norse myths are bleaker than the Greek and Roman tales. Norse gods live in a high plane called Asgard, where they await the inevitable doom that faces them in the battle that will end the world—a reflection of the pessimistic Norse belief that good will eventually lose to evil. Heroism exists, defined by fighting for good in the face of certain defeat and dying in the attempt. Dead heroes are honored in Valhalla, the afterlife for good warriors, where they sit with gods in Asgard who, like them, face defeat in the end.

## Summary: Chapter I — The Stories of Signy and Sigurd

The Volsung dynasty's story is told in the *Volsungasaga* as well as in the *Elder Edda*. Signy, a daughter of Volsung, marries an evil man who kills her father, then imprisons and kills all her brothers except Sigmund, whom she is able to rescue. To procure Sigmund a comrade for the vengeance they are planning, Signy disguises herself and spends three nights with her brother and conceives a child. While the boy, Sinfiotli, grows up, Signy keeps quiet and pretends to love her husband. When Sinfiotli comes of age, he and Sigmund kill Signy's husband and all his children by burning them in a locked house. Seeing her wish done, Signy herself walks into the burning building to die with the family she has killed.

Sigmund later has a son named Sigurd, who braves a ring of fire to free the imprisoned maiden Brynhild, a Valkyrie who has disobeyed Odin, the lord of the gods. Sigurd and Brynhild pledge their love for each other. He leaves her in the same ring of fire, intending to return, and visits his best friend, the king Gunnar. Gunnar's mother, who wants Sigurd to marry her own daughter, Gudrun, gives Sigurd a potion that makes him forget Brynhild.

Gunnar decides he wants Brynhild for a wife, but he is unable to pass the marriage-test of the ring of fire. Sigurd rides through the flames again disguised as Gunnar and wins Brynhild for his friend. Brynhild marries Gunnar, thinking he legitimately passed the test and assuming Sigurd abandoned her. When she learns the truth, she falls into a rage of vengeance and falsely convinces Gunnar that Sigurd slept with her when he rescued her from the ring of fire. Gunnar persuades his younger brother to kill Sigurd. After Sigurd's death, Brynhild kills herself, asking to be placed on the funeral pyre next to him.

## Summary: Chapter II — The Norse Gods

### *The Creation*

Odin, the chief Norse gods, rules Asgard from Gladsheim, his palace, attended by the Valkyries and leading the gods in their constant battle against the Giants of Jotunheim. A strange, taciturn god, Odin eats nothing himself but gives his food to his two pet wolves under the banquet table. His two ravens, Thought and Memory, scour the world for news, on which he meditates while the other gods feast. Concerned with wisdom, Odin once gave up one of his own eyes and hung for nine days and nights from a tree in order to gain it. Odin gives this wisdom, along with the Runes—the old Norse written alphabet that has magical powers—and the special liquor that transforms its drinker into a poet, to the race of men.

There are five other great gods besides Odin: Balder, Thor, Freyr, Heimdall, and Tyr. Thor is the thunder-bearer and strongest of the gods; Freyr is the god of the crops; Heimdall is the guardian of the rainbow-bridge between Asgard and the world of men; and Tyr is the god of war. There are three major goddesses—Frigga (Odin's wife), Freya, and Hela—but they are not important to Norse myth. Frigga is an indistinct figure, a spinner of secret thread; Freya, like Aphrodite, is a goddess of love; and Hela is queen of the underworld.

In one story, Frigga learns that her son Balder is fated to die. In a panic, she persuades every animate and inanimate object on earth never to harm him. They all agree, because Balder is so beloved. But Frigga forgets to ask the mistletoe plant. The other gods make a game of Balder's invulnerability, throwing things at him because nothing hurts him. The evil deity Loki tricks Frigga into revealing the one object in the world that might harm Balder. Loki convinces Hoder, Balder's blind brother, to throw a mistletoe dart at Balder. Loki guides it to pierce Balder's heart. Hela agrees to bring Balder back to life if it can be proved that everything everywhere mourns his passing, but one recalcitrant ogress refuses to show sorrow for Balder. Balder, therefore, must remain with the dead. As punishment, Loki is chained to a rock in a deep cavern, where a serpent is placed over his head that drips burning venom on his face.

### *The Norse Wisdom*

In the beginning of the Norse universe, there is only an empty chasm surrounded by Niflheim, the cold realm of death in the north, and Muspelheim, the land of fire in the south. Cold and fire combine in the chasm to form Ymir, the first Giant and grandfather of Odin. Odin and his two brothers kill Ymir and make the heavens from his skull, the sea from his blood, and the earth—Misgard, humankind's realm—from his body. The gigantic ash-tree Yggdrasil supports the universe. One of its roots goes up to Asgard, and beside it lies the sacred Urda's well, guarded by the three Norns, who, like the Greek Fates, allot lifespans and destinies to men. A serpent gnaws at the roots of Yggdrasil; when he gnaws all the way through, the tree and the universe will topple. The serpent symbolizes Ragnarok, the inevitable doomsday that ends the universe, when even the gods meet destruction as evil vanquishes good. Eventually, a new good god will rise up and rid the world of evil forever. In addition to myths, the *Elder Edda* also contains a wealth of proverbs and insights about all manner of aspects of human life, from insomnia to irony.

## Analysis: Part Seven

Hamilton's inclusion of Norse mythology broadens her narrative, but, by current thinking, her reasons for including it are outdated. She writes that the Norse myths are the legacy of "the whole great Teutonic race" and that "by race we are connected to the Norse." Though Hamilton has valid points, her Eurocentric perspective is anachronistic in the multicultural America of today. Though her perspective may be archaic, the brief glimpse of the compelling themes and ideas of Norse myth that she provides is valuable. We see a counterpoint to the Greek and Roman myths, a world with different meanings and symbols. The Norse gods maintain far more gravity than the classical deities: their stories are never frivolous, self-conscious, or shallow, but rather compelling and provocative.

The idea of Ragnarok, a doomsday when even the gods are fated to die, is unique to the Norse worldview—a cold and bleak outlook, perhaps a reflection of the harsh northern life that the Vikings led. Loki, the wicked demi-god trickster, is unlike anyone in Greek myth. Odin, the chief god, is likewise an unusual figure: in some respects he is Christ-like—with his self-imposed crucifixion from a tree in order to gain wisdom for humankind—yet also removed and withdrawn, with ravens and wolves for companions. Odin is devastatingly serious at all times, aware of the inevitability of Ragnarok and his own responsibility to delay it as long as possible.

# Important Quotations Explained

1.  Here Phaëthon lies, who drove the Sun-god's car.
    Greatly he failed, but he had greatly dared.

In Part Two, Chapter IV, Hamilton tells the story of Phaëthon, the son of the Sun-god by a mortal woman. The doubtful Phaëthon goes to visit the Sun to verify his parentage and ends up joyriding on the Sun's chariot, only to be shot down after losing control of it. Like Icarus, who flies too high on wings of wax only to have them melt, Phaëthon is an archetypal case of overreaching one's place by an act of reckless arrogance. Tragedy inevitably befalls those mortals who confuse their position and worth with those of the gods.

Yet these two brief lines also contain a second, brilliant counterpoint to the lesson of humility in the story of Phaëthon's tragic mistake. If the first line demonstrates the ill fate that overtakes him for overstepping himself, the second line subtly heroizes him. Phaëthon falls into disaster, but has striven equally far for greatness. As much as Greek and Roman myths caution humans against arrogance, they also pique our curiosity at, and celebrate those who have achieved, dazzling and original acts of triumph.

2.  [I]f I must slay
    The joy of my house, my daughter.
    A father's hands
    Stained with dark streams flowing
    From blood of a girl
    Slaughtered before the altar.

Agamemnon speaks these anguished words—quoted from Aeschylus in Part Four, Chapter I—after learning that the Greek ships cannot sail for Troy unless his daughter, Iphigenia, is sacrificed to appease the angry Artemis. Though the very idea of the act is ghastly and repulsive to him, Agamemnon follows through with it, as it seems the only honorable way to perform his duty to his fellow Greeks and uphold the oath he has sworn to help his brother Menelaus reclaim his wife, Helen. Agamemnon's allegiance is with his social brotherhood more than his family, for he feels the dishonor of preventing the Greeks from sailing is greater than the dishonor of murdering his own child. Already, Agamemnon couches his response as something he "must" do, not as something asked of him. He believes that any mandated duty to a god is justified, even if it is entails a horrible crime like murdering one's own daughter.

Clytemnestra, Agamemnon's wife, takes a violently different view when he returns home, slaughtering him in revenge. Yet paradoxically, the very principle by which Clytemnestra justifies her action is the same upon which Agamemnon based his, because she obviously feels the duty of avenging her daughter outweighs the crime of killing one's own husband. With this quote, thus, we see both the theme of the self-perpetuating nature of bloodshed as well as the complexity of the moral dilemmas that formed the subject of much Greek tragedy.

3. We stand at the same point of pain.
   We too are slaves.
   Our children are crying, calling to us with tears, "Mother, I am all alone.
   To the dark ships now they drive me,
   And I cannot see you, Mother."

These lines, spoken in Euripides' *The Trojan Women* at the fall of Troy, appear in Part Four, Chapter II. True to the sophistication of the Greek playwrights, Euripides does not, in his consideration of the Trojan War, rest with a simple glorification of the Greek military victory. Rather, he depicts the useless devastation and catastrophe that war brings alongside its glory. We feel the sorrow of the innocent—a sorrow infinitely multiplied when we recall that the only cause of the war is a spat over the lovely Helen.

Although Homer's *Iliad* does not address the sophisticated aftermath of the Trojan War in the way that *The Trojan Women* does, the *Iliad* does portray the conflict as more than just a simple struggle between good and evil. We see heroism, strength of character, wisdom, and honor on both the Greek and Trojan sides. The *Iliad* ends with the death of Hector, the brave Trojan, portraying his loss as a great tragedy equal to the tragic death of the Greek Achilles. Both Euripides' play and Homer's epic depict humans caught in a web of circumstances beyond their control, facing their difficult situations and making the only ethical decisions possible, even when the clear consequence is death. The quotation, then, captures this moral complexity of war with an insightful snapshot of the human condition beyond the glory and spoils of a proud battle.

4. "What creature," the Sphinx asked him, "goes on four feet in the morning, on two at noonday, on three in the evening?"

The answer Oedipus gives, in Part Five, Chapter II, is "[m]an." As a baby, man crawls; in maturity, he walks upright on his two feet; near the end of his life, he walks with a cane. Answering this riddle, Oedipus saves the city of Thebes from the curse of the Sphinx, who kills herself. Oedipus does not, however, realize the implications the riddle has for his own life.

At this point, Oedipus is chronologically between the two major criminal acts that make up his tragedy, though he commits them unknowingly. He has just killed his father, Laius, and he is about to—again unwittingly—marry his mother Jocasta. These actions divide Oedipus's life into three stages of its own. First is the early part of his life in which he grows up as the adopted son of Polybus, from whom he flees in order to avoid fulfilling an oracle's prophecy and committing patricide. Second is his triumphal stage, as he becomes king of Thebes and marries its widowed queen, Jocasta, after defeating the Sphinx. Third is his blinded stage, as it is revealed that Jocasta is his mother and that he has inadvertently slain his true father, Laius, on his flight from Polybus. We see that Oedipus's life itself corresponds to the Sphinx's riddle. At his birth, his true parents abandon him because of another prophecy, and he is forced to rely on the kindness of Polybus. At the second stage, when man stands erect, Oedipus finds himself on top of the Theban world, glorified as a hero, deemed a king, and married with children. The last stage, when man needs a cane to aid his lameness in walking, corresponds to Oedipus's self-inflicted blindness, when he is disappointed and impaired but still alive to continue the last leg of his journey.

5. [The Roman race] left to other nations such things as art and science, and ever remembered that they were destined to bring under their empire the peoples of earth, to impose the rule of submissive nonresistance, to spare the humbled and to crush the proud.

Hamilton ends her account of the *Aeneid* in Part Four, Chapter IV, with this strange declaration of Virgil on the nature of "the Roman race." In order to understand it, we should bear in mind both the legacy to which Virgil is responding as well as the contemporary backdrop to which he addresses himself. The original Romans had a very indistinct and undeveloped religious worldview, in which deities were little more than barely personified forces. As a result, the Romans responded well to the colorful and engaging body of stories the Greeks had compiled. Consequently, when the Romans came in greater and greater contact with the Greeks, they took over the entire Greek system, only bothering to change some names to harmonize the new gods with existing traditions. They also adopted Greek philosophy, science, and artistic practices.

With so much cultural and intellectual matter adopted from another race, the Romans suffered a lingering void in their national identity. To counter the impression of such an absence, the Romans turned to the areas in which their own culture excelled. In Virgil's time, the Romans had military prowess and a strong, organized state. The current emperor, Augustus, had expanded and consolidated the geographic possessions of Rome into an empire of unprecedented scope and status. Virgil's remark is rather defensive, implying that the Romans had voluntarily laid aside the projects of art and science—no doubt to the Greeks, as well as to other civilizations—in favor of achieving world dominance. Interestingly, the last part of Virgil's statement almost likens the Romans' role to that of the gods in describing them as arbiters of humility and pride. In fact, Augustus initiated a long tradition among emperors by deifying the deceased Julius Caesar, officially declaring him a god and forcing the empire's subjects to worship him.

# Key Facts

**FULL TITLE**
*Mythology*

**AUTHOR**
Edith Hamilton

**TYPE OF WORK**
Nonfiction

**GENRE**
Classical lore and legends, Norse legends

**LANGUAGE**
English

**TIME AND PLACE WRITTEN**
1930s, United States

**DATE OF FIRST PUBLICATION**
1942

**PUBLISHER**
Little, Brown and Company

**NARRATOR**
An omniscient narrator, suggestive of the author herself

**POINT OF VIEW**
Edith Hamilton's level and even-spirited scholarly voice provides the general point of view. The stories are told by omniscient narrators who are sympathetic to the protagonists yet instantly aware of their weaknesses or foolishness whenever it comes into play. Even these omniscient narrators have plenty of equanimity and are not terribly engaged in the stories they are telling.

**TONE**
Edith Hamilton clearly admires the greatness of antiquity, although at the same time posits myths as important mostly as progenitors of "us" and "our culture."

**TENSE**
Past

**SETTING (TIME)**
Ancient times

**SETTING (PLACE)**
Greece and Rome, and, at the very end, Northern Europe

**THEMES**
The dominance of fate; bloodshed begets bloodshed; the danger of arrogance and hubris; reward for goodness and retribution for evil

**MOTIFS**
The hero's quest; beauty; love

**SYMBOLS**
Cannibalism; art

# Study Questions

1.  *Compare and contrast the characters of Odysseus and Aeneas. How do the aspects of their heroism differ? What does this say about their respective societies?*

Odysseus is the prototypical Greek hero; Aeneas is the prototypical Roman hero. Both are brave and unwaveringly committed to triumph over adversity, completion of goals, and obedience to the gods. In their differences, however, they demonstrate the values of their respective societies. The crafty Odysseus's greatest exploits—devising the Trojan Horse, defeating Polyphemus, destroying Penelope's suitors—involve cunning and plotting. He seems more human in his concern for his men, his susceptibility to temptation, his recognition of his limited mortal strength, and his reliance on his wits. He represents the Greek ideal of the intellectual warrior who possesses a delicate, almost artistic appreciation of love and friendship.

Aeneas, on the other hand, is first and foremost a warrior, the model soldier. He rejects the love of Dido in the service of duty: the accomplishment of his destiny is to found a great empire. By the end, he becomes superhuman in strength and wisdom—far from the crafty deception that enables Odysseus to survive. Aeneas is indeed much more in line with the Roman virtues of military strength and forcefulness of character.

2.  *Compare and contrast the visions of heroism in the* Iliad *and the* Odyssey. *How do these visions reflect different ideas about human life and its place in the world?*

The *Iliad* has no primary antagonist: there are warriors on both sides who are heroic, most notably the Trojan Hector and the Greek Achilles. The *Iliad* thus portrays a world in which all human participants are locked in a struggle against a vague and inevitable evil. The focus is on the web of circumstances in which humans are caught and the challenges set forth by the virtues—honor, bravery, and loyalty—that should govern relations in a social community. It is like a manual for an ideal, ethical Greek society, yet also rather foreign to us, with superhuman heroes who follow strange rules of honor and custom.

The *Odyssey,* on the other hand, depicts a heroism and a challenge to which we can relate. Rather than a single-minded, iron warrior, Odysseus relies on his shrewdness and wit to get out of trouble. He humanly falls prey to temptations, staying too long in his revels with Circe. The greatest danger—the one that permeates the whole epic—is one that we all face: the danger of forgetting, in a restless search for beauty and experience, our mundane responsibilities and those to whom we owe. We are not concerned with Odysseus's battle against the enemy in war but rather his battle against the forces that keep him away from his family and home in Ithaca.

3. *Discuss the ways in which these myths functioned as literature, science, and religion.*

As literature, the myths offer complex, engaging, and often amusing entertainment. Even the brutal stories of Oedipus and Orestes became famous plays designed to engage a viewing audience. The scientific aspect of the myths is most visible in those that attempt to explain certain phenomena—the stories of Pyramus and Thisbe (why mulberries are red), Procne and Philomela (why the swallow has no song), and Hercules at Gibraltar (how the Rock of Gibraltar appeared) are classic examples. In a broader sense, the world of the Olympians offered general explanations for the mysteries of the universe. The ground is barren in winter because Demeter is mourning. Lightning occurs when Zeus is angry. More generally, strange, sad and undeservedly bad things happen because it is merely the nature of the gods or the decree of the Fate.

The myths also try to answer a question that straddles the line between religion and science. The religious aspect of the myths is obvious: most myths illustrate concepts of morality, showing what pleases the gods and what upsets them. In this world, morality is cast in religious terms. Finally, most of the best known myths—like those of Theseus, Hercules, Jason and the Golden Fleece, the Trojan War, Oedipus, and Orestes—deal with the cruelty and pain that even the greatest heroes face. Such stories make sense of the world's senseless cruelty, demonstrating that, for whatever reason, the gods necessarily maintain a place for suffering in the world.

# How to Write Literary Analysis

## The Literary Essay: A Step-by-Step Guide

When you read for pleasure, your only goal is enjoyment. You might find yourself reading to get caught up in an exciting story, to learn about an interesting time or place, or just to pass time. Maybe you're looking for inspiration, guidance, or a reflection of your own life. There are as many different, valid ways of reading a book as there are books in the world.

When you read a work of literature in an English class, however, you're being asked to read in a special way: you're being asked to perform *literary analysis*. To analyze something means to break it down into smaller parts and then examine how those parts work, both individually and together. Literary analysis involves examining all the parts of a novel, play, short story, or poem—elements such as character, setting, tone, and imagery—and thinking about how the author uses those elements to create certain effects.

A literary essay isn't a book review: you're not being asked whether or not you liked a book or whether you'd recommend it to another reader. A literary essay also isn't like the kind of book report you wrote when you were younger, where your teacher wanted you to summarize the book's action. A high school- or college-level literary essay asks, "How does this piece of literature actually work?" "How does it do what it does?" and, "Why might the author have made the choices he or she did?"

### The Seven Steps
No one is born knowing how to analyze literature; it's a skill you learn and a process you can master. As you gain more practice with this kind of thinking and writing, you'll be able to craft a method that works best for you. But until then, here are seven basic steps to writing a well-constructed literary essay:

*1. Ask questions*
*2. Collect evidence*
*3. Construct a thesis*

*4. Develop and organize arguments*
*5. Write the introduction*
*6. Write the body paragraphs*
*7. Write the conclusion*

---

## 1. Ask Questions

When you're assigned a literary essay in class, your teacher will often provide you with a list of writing prompts. Lucky you! Now all you have to do is choose one. Do yourself a favor and pick a topic that interests you. You'll have a much better (not to mention easier) time if you start off with something you enjoy thinking about. If you are asked to come up with a topic by yourself, though, you might start to feel a little panicked. Maybe you have too many ideas—or none at all. Don't worry. Take a deep breath and start by asking yourself these questions:

- **What struck you?** Did a particular image, line, or scene linger in your mind for a long time? If it fascinated you, chances are you can draw on it to write a fascinating essay.
- **What confused you?** Maybe you were surprised to see a character act in a certain way, or maybe you didn't understand why the book ended the way it did. Confusing moments in a work of literature are like a loose thread in a sweater: if you pull on it, you can unravel the entire thing. Ask yourself why the author chose to write about that character or scene the way he or she did and you might tap into some important insights about the work as a whole.
- **Did you notice any patterns?** Is there a phrase that the main character uses constantly or an image that repeats throughout the book? If you can figure out how that pattern weaves through the work and what the significance of that pattern is, you've almost got your entire essay mapped out.
- **Did you notice any contradictions or ironies?** Great works of literature are complex; great literary essays recognize and explain those complexities. Maybe the title (*Happy Days*) totally disagrees with the book's subject matter (hungry orphans dying in the woods). Maybe the main character acts one way around his family and a completely different way around his friends and associates. If you can find a way to explain a work's contradictory elements, you've got the seeds of a great essay.

At this point, you don't need to know exactly what you're going to say about your topic; you just need a place to begin your exploration. You can help direct your reading and brainstorming by formulating your topic as a *question,* which you'll then try to answer in your essay. The best questions invite critical debates and discussions, not just a rehashing of the summary. Remember, you're looking for something you can *prove or argue* based on evidence you find in the text. Finally, remember to keep the scope of your question in mind: is this a topic you can adequately address within the word or page limit you've been given? Conversely, is this a topic big enough to fill the required length?

### GOOD QUESTIONS

> *"Are Romeo and Juliet's parents responsible for the deaths of their children?"*
> *"Why do pigs keep showing up in* LORD OF THE FLIES*?"*
> *"Are Dr. Frankenstein and his monster alike? How?"*

### BAD QUESTIONS

> *"What happens to Scout in* TO KILL A MOCKINGBIRD*?"*
> *"What do the other characters in* JULIUS CAESAR *think about Caesar?"*
> *"How does Hester Prynne in* THE SCARLET LETTER *remind me of my sister?"*

---

### 2. COLLECT EVIDENCE

Once you know what question you want to answer, it's time to scour the book for things that will help you answer the question. Don't worry if you don't know what you want to say yet—right now you're just collecting ideas and material and letting it all percolate. Keep track of passages, symbols, images, or scenes that deal with your topic. Eventually, you'll start making connections between these examples and your thesis will emerge.

Here's a brief summary of the various parts that compose each and every work of literature. These are the elements that you will analyze in your essay, and which you will offer as evidence to support your arguments. For more on the parts of literary works, see the Glossary of Literary Terms at the end of this section.

ELEMENTS OF STORY   These are the *what*s of the work—what happens, where it happens, and to whom it happens.

- **Plot:** All of the events and actions of the work.
- **Character:** The people who act and are acted upon in a literary work. The main character of a work is known as the *protagonist*.
- **Conflict:** The central tension in the work. In most cases, the protagonist wants something, while opposing forces (antagonists) hinder the protagonist's progress.
- **Setting:** When and where the work takes place. Elements of setting include location, time period, time of day, weather, social atmosphere, and economic conditions.
- **Narrator:** The person telling the story. The narrator may straightforwardly report what happens, convey the subjective opinions and perceptions of one or more characters, or provide commentary and opinion in his or her own voice.
- **Themes:** The main idea or message of the work—usually an abstract idea about people, society, or life in general. A work may have many themes, which may be in tension with one another.

ELEMENTS OF STYLE   These are the *how*s—how the characters speak, how the story is constructed, and how language is used throughout the work.

- **Structure and organization:** How the parts of the work are assembled. Some novels are narrated in a linear, chronological fashion, while others skip around in time. Some plays follow a traditional three- or five-act structure, while others are a series of loosely connected scenes. Some authors deliberately leave gaps in their works, leaving readers to puzzle out the missing information. A work's structure and organization can tell you a lot about the kind of message it wants to convey.
- **Point of view:** The perspective from which a story is told. In *first-person point of view*, the narrator involves him or herself in the story. ("I went to the store"; "We watched in horror as the bird slammed into the window.") A first-person narrator is usually the protagonist of the work, but not always. In *third-person point of view*, the narrator does not participate

in the story. A third-person narrator may closely follow a specific character, recounting that individual character's thoughts or experiences, or it may be what we call an *omniscient* narrator. Omniscient narrators see and know all: they can witness any event in any time or place and are privy to the inner thoughts and feelings of all characters. Remember that the narrator and the author are not the same thing!

- **Diction:** Word choice. Whether a character uses dry, clinical language or flowery prose with lots of exclamation points can tell you a lot about his or her attitude and personality.
- **Syntax:** Word order and sentence construction. Syntax is a crucial part of establishing an author's narrative voice. Ernest Hemingway, for example, is known for writing in very short, straightforward sentences, while James Joyce characteristically wrote in long, incredibly complicated lines.
- **Tone:** The mood or feeling of the text. Diction and syntax often contribute to the tone of a work. A novel written in short, clipped sentences that use small, simple words might feel brusque, cold, or matter-of-fact.
- **Imagery:** Language that appeals to the senses, representing things that can be seen, smelled, heard, tasted, or touched.
- **Figurative language:** Language that is not meant to be interpreted literally. The most common types of figurative language are *metaphors* and *similes,* which compare two unlike things in order to suggest a similarity between them—for example, "All the world's a stage," or "The moon is like a ball of green cheese." (Metaphors say one thing *is* another thing; similes claim that one thing is *like* another thing.)

## 3. Construct a Thesis

When you've examined all the evidence you've collected and know how you want to answer the question, it's time to write your thesis statement. A *thesis* is a claim about a work of literature that needs to be supported by evidence and arguments. The thesis statement is the heart of the literary essay, and the bulk of your paper will be spent trying to prove this claim. A good thesis will be:

- **Arguable.** "*The Great Gatsby* describes New York society in the 1920s" isn't a thesis—it's a fact.

- **Provable through textual evidence**. "*Hamlet* is a confusing but ultimately very well-written play" is a weak thesis because it offers the writer's personal opinion about the book. Yes, it's arguable, but it's not a claim that can be proved or supported with examples taken from the play itself.
- **Surprising**. "Both George and Lenny change a great deal in *Of Mice and Men*" is a weak thesis because it's obvious. A really strong thesis will argue for a reading of the text that is not immediately apparent.
- **Specific**. "Dr. Frankenstein's monster tells us a lot about the human condition" is *almost* a really great thesis statement, but it's still too vague. What does the writer mean by "a lot"? *How* does the monster tell us so much about the human condition?

## Good Thesis Statements

**Question:** In *Romeo and Juliet*, which is more powerful in shaping the lovers' story: fate or foolishness?

**Thesis:** "Though Shakespeare defines Romeo and Juliet as 'star-crossed lovers' and images of stars and planets appear throughout the play, a closer examination of that celestial imagery reveals that the stars are merely witnesses to the characters' foolish activities and not the causes themselves."

**Question:** How does the bell jar function as a symbol in Sylvia Plath's *The Bell Jar*?

**Thesis:** "A bell jar is a bell-shaped glass that has three basic uses: to hold a specimen for observation, to contain gases, and to maintain a vacuum. The bell jar appears in each of these capacities in *The Bell Jar*, Plath's semi-autobiographical novel, and each appearance marks a different stage in Esther's mental breakdown."

**Question:** Would Piggy in *The Lord of the Flies* make a good island leader if he were given the chance?

**Thesis:** "Though the intelligent, rational, and innovative Piggy has the mental characteristics of a good leader, he ultimately lacks the social skills necessary to be an effective one. Golding emphasizes this point by giving Piggy a foil in the charismatic Jack, whose magnetic personality allows him to capture and wield power effectively, if not always wisely."

### 4. Develop and Organize Arguments

The reasons and examples that support your thesis will form the middle paragraphs of your essay. Since you can't really write your thesis statement until you know how you'll structure your argument, you'll probably end up working on steps 3 and 4 at the same time.

There's no single method of argumentation that will work in every context. One essay prompt might ask you to compare and contrast two characters, while another asks you to trace an image through a given work of literature. These questions require different kinds of answers and therefore different kinds of arguments. Below, we'll discuss three common kinds of essay prompts and some strategies for constructing a solid, well-argued case.

### Types of Literary Essays

- **Compare and contrast**

    *Compare and contrast the characters of Huck and Jim in* THE ADVENTURES OF HUCKLEBERRY FINN.

    Chances are you've written this kind of essay before. In an academic literary context, you'll organize your arguments the same way you would in any other class. You can either go *subject by subject* or *point by point*. In the former, you'll discuss one character first and then the second. In the latter, you'll choose several traits (attitude toward life, social status, images and metaphors associated with the character) and devote a paragraph to each. You may want to use a mix of these two approaches—for example, you may want to spend a paragraph a piece broadly sketching Huck's and Jim's personalities before transitioning into a paragraph or two that describes a few key points of comparison. This can be a highly effective strategy if you want to make a counterintuitive argument—that, despite seeming to be totally different, the two objects being compared are actually similar in a very important way (or vice versa). Remember that your essay should reveal something fresh or unexpected about the text, so think beyond the obvious parallels and differences.

- **Trace**

    *Choose an image—for example, birds, knives, or eyes—and trace that image throughout* MACBETH.

    Sounds pretty easy, right? All you need to do is read the play, underline every appearance of a knife in *Macbeth,* and then list them in your essay in the order they appear, right? Well, not exactly. Your teacher doesn't want a simple catalog of examples. He or she wants to see you make *connections* between those examples—that's the difference between summarizing and analyzing. In the *Macbeth* example above, think about the different contexts in which knives appear in the play and to what effect. In *Macbeth,* there are real knives and imagined knives; knives that kill and knives that simply threaten. Categorize and classify your examples to give them some order. Finally, always keep the overall effect in mind. After you choose and analyze your examples, you should come to some greater understanding about the work, as well as your chosen image, symbol, or phrase's role in developing the major themes and stylistic strategies of that work.

- **Debate**

    *Is the society depicted in 1984 good for its citizens?*

    In this kind of essay, you're being asked to debate a moral, ethical, or aesthetic issue regarding the work. You might be asked to judge a character or group of characters (*Is Caesar responsible for his own demise?*) or the work itself (*Is* JANE EYRE *a feminist novel?*). For this kind of essay, there are two important points to keep in mind. First, don't simply base your arguments on your personal feelings and reactions. Every literary essay expects you to read and analyze the work, so search for evidence in the text. What do characters in *1984* have to say about the government of Oceania? What images does Orwell use that might give you a hint about his attitude toward the government? As in any debate, you also need to make sure that you define all the necessary terms before you begin to argue your case. What does it mean to be a "good" society? What makes a novel "feminist"? You should define your terms right up front, in the first paragraph after your introduction.

    Second, remember that strong literary essays make contrary and surprising arguments. Try to think outside the box. In the *1984* example above, it seems like the obvious answer would be no, the totalitarian society depicted in Orwell's novel is *not* good for its citizens. But can you think of any arguments for the opposite side? Even if your final assertion is that the novel depicts a cruel, repressive, and therefore harmful society, acknowledging and responding to the counterargument will strengthen your overall case.

5. Write the Introduction

Your introduction sets up the entire essay. It's where you present your topic and articulate the particular issues and questions you'll be addressing. It's also where you, as the writer, introduce yourself to your readers. A persuasive literary essay immediately establishes its writer as a knowledgeable, authoritative figure.

An introduction can vary in length depending on the overall length of the essay, but in a traditional five-paragraph essay it should be no longer than one paragraph. However long it is, your introduction needs to:

- **Provide any necessary context.** Your introduction should situate the reader and let him or her know what to expect. What book are you discussing? Which characters? What topic will you be addressing?

- **Answer the "So what?" question.** Why is this topic important, and why is your particular position on the topic noteworthy? Ideally, your introduction should pique the reader's interest by suggesting how your argument is surprising or otherwise counterintuitive. Literary essays make unexpected connections and reveal less-than-obvious truths.

- **Present your thesis.** This usually happens at or very near the end of your introduction.

- **Indicate the shape of the essay to come.** Your reader should finish reading your introduction with a good sense of the scope of your essay as well as the path you'll take toward proving your thesis. You don't need to spell out every step, but you do need to suggest the organizational pattern you'll be using.

Your introduction should not:

- **Be vague.** Beware of the two killer words in literary analysis: *interesting* and *important*. Of course the work, question, or example is interesting and important—that's why you're writing about it!

- **Open with any grandiose assertions.** Many student readers think that beginning their essays with a flamboyant statement such as, "Since the dawn of time, writers have been fascinated with the topic of free will," makes them sound important and commanding. You know what? It actually sounds pretty amateurish.

- **Wildly praise the work.** Another typical mistake student writers make is extolling the work or author. Your teacher doesn't need to be told that "Shakespeare is perhaps the greatest writer in the English language." You can mention a work's reputation in passing—by referring to *The Adventures of Huckleberry Finn* as "Mark Twain's enduring classic," for example—but don't make a point of bringing it up unless that reputation is key to your argument.
- **Go off-topic.** Keep your introduction streamlined and to the point. Don't feel the need to throw in all kinds of bells and whistles in order to impress your reader—just get to the point as quickly as you can, without skimping on any of the required steps.

### 6. Write the Body Paragraphs

Once you've written your introduction, you'll take the arguments you developed in step 4 and turn them into your body paragraphs. The organization of this middle section of your essay will largely be determined by the argumentative strategy you use, but no matter how you arrange your thoughts, your body paragraphs need to do the following:

- **Begin with a strong topic sentence.** Topic sentences are like signs on a highway: they tell the reader where they are and where they're going. A good topic sentence not only alerts readers to what issue will be discussed in the following paragraph but also gives them a sense of what argument will be made *about* that issue. "Rumor and gossip play an important role in *The Crucible*" isn't a strong topic sentence because it doesn't tell us very much. "The community's constant gossiping creates an environment that allows false accusations to flourish" is a much stronger topic sentence—it not only tells us *what* the paragraph will discuss (gossip) but *how* the paragraph will discuss the topic (by showing how gossip creates a set of conditions that leads to the play's climactic action).
- **Fully and completely develop a single thought.** Don't skip around in your paragraph or try to stuff in too much material. Body paragraphs are like bricks: each individual

one needs to be strong and sturdy or the entire structure will collapse. Make sure you have really proven your point before moving on to the next one.

- **Use transitions effectively.** Good literary essay writers know that each paragraph must be clearly and strongly linked to the material around it. Think of each paragraph as a response to the one that precedes it. Use transition words and phrases such as *however, similarly, on the contrary, therefore,* and *furthermore* to indicate what kind of response you're making.

7. WRITE THE CONCLUSION

Just as you used the introduction to ground your readers in the topic before providing your thesis, you'll use the conclusion to quickly summarize the specifics learned thus far and then hint at the broader implications of your topic. A good conclusion will:

- **Do more than simply restate the thesis.** If your thesis argued that *The Catcher in the Rye* can be read as a Christian allegory, don't simply end your essay by saying, "And that is why *The Catcher in the Rye* can be read as a Christian allegory." If you've constructed your arguments well, this kind of statement will just be redundant.

- **Synthesize the arguments, not summarize them.** Similarly, don't repeat the details of your body paragraphs in your conclusion. The reader has already read your essay, and chances are it's not so long that they've forgotten all your points by now.

- **Revisit the "So what?" question.** In your introduction, you made a case for why your topic and position are important. You should close your essay with the same sort of gesture. What do your readers know now that they didn't know before? How will that knowledge help them better appreciate or understand the work overall?

- **Move from the specific to the general.** Your essay has most likely treated a very specific element of the work—a single character, a small set of images, or a particular passage. In your conclusion, try to show how this narrow discussion has wider implications for the work overall. If your essay on *To Kill a Mockingbird* focused on the character of Boo Radley, for example, you might want to include a bit in your conclusion about how he fits into the novel's larger message about childhood, innocence, or family life.

- **Stay relevant.**  Your conclusion should suggest new directions of thought, but it shouldn't be treated as an opportunity to pad your essay with all the extra, interesting ideas you came up with during your brainstorming sessions but couldn't fit into the essay proper. Don't attempt to stuff in unrelated queries or too many abstract thoughts.

- **Avoid making overblown closing statements.**  A conclusion should open up your highly specific, focused discussion, but it should do so without drawing a sweeping lesson about life or human nature. Making such observations may be part of the point of reading, but it's almost always a mistake in essays, where these observations tend to sound overly dramatic or simply silly.

---

### A+ Essay Checklist

Congratulations! If you've followed all the steps we've outlined above, you should have a solid literary essay to show for all your efforts. What if you've got your sights set on an A+? To write the kind of superlative essay that will be rewarded with a perfect grade, keep the following rubric in mind. These are the qualities that teachers expect to see in a truly A+ essay. How does yours stack up?

- ✓ Demonstrates a thorough understanding of the book
- ✓ Presents an original, compelling argument
- ✓ Thoughtfully analyzes the text's formal elements
- ✓ Uses appropriate and insightful examples
- ✓ Structures ideas in a logical and progressive order
- ✓ Demonstrates a mastery of sentence construction, transitions, grammar, spelling, and word choice

## Suggested Essay Topics

1. *In terms of the myths as a whole, what is unusual about Hercules' character? How does he maintain his heroic stature after committing so many crimes?*

2. *Neither Oedipus, nor Orestes, nor Antigone goes on any long adventure full of monsters and vicious gods, yet all three are considered "heroes" of Greek myth. What defines these three unusual characters as heroic?*

3. *Compare and contrast the stories of Orestes and Medea. Both are about vengeance, but why is one character celebrated and the other demonized?*

4. *Prometheus is an unusual character—among other reasons, for defying both his fellow Titans and, later, Zeus. What do you make of his actions? As what kind of symbol might he have functioned for the classical authors?*

5. *The myths are full of instances of the cruelty of the gods. Giving multiple examples, discuss the reasons for the gods' cruelty. Is it always justified? What does the cruelty of the gods say about the Greeks' view of the universe?*

# A+ Student Essay

*Choose one myth and explore the relationships between its male and female characters. What broader arguments might be drawn from these examples?*

"The Adventures of Aeneas" is mainly concerned with its titular male hero, the Trojan founder of Rome. However, the tale also features several women in key supporting roles, such as Juno, Venus, and Dido. As in many of the other classical stories recounted in Hamilton's book, "The Adventures of Aeneas" seems to emphasize women's passivity and their inability to directly alter their circumstances, as men may. However, the tale also includes several examples of how females may exercise power and even hints that, by rejecting men, women might wield even greater power than they currently do.

Though both Juno and Venus are divine and powerful goddesses, "The Adventures of Aeneas"—particularly the first part—emphasizes how neither goddess affects Aeneas's fate directly. Instead, both rely on traditionally feminine methods of manipulation to convince male gods to act on their behalf. In her first attempt to stop Aeneas, Juno bargains with Aeolus, the King of the Winds, to sink the Trojan ships. Although Aeolus is technically a lesser deity than Juno, she still must resort to bribery in order to win his compliance. By contrast, Juno's brother Neptune simply reprimands Aeolus and calms the sea, making it possible for the Trojans to reach land. Juno is thus presented as a female goddess who relies on persuasion and trickery and is strongly countered by an active male god. Like Juno, Venus cannot exercise her power directly; she too relies on securing the favors of male gods. When Juno plots to have Aeneas fall in love with Dido so that he will abandon his journey, Venus counters her by employing the help of her son, Cupid, and Juno's own husband, Jupiter. She uses her divine beauty and feminine appeal to extract promises from both males to help Aeneas.

However, despite the roundabout ways in which the dueling goddesses achieve their goals—methods that would be derided in a culture so committed to direct, forceful action—it cannot be denied that their techniques are effective. Or, for that matter, that the most ferocious agent of the goddesses' desires is herself a female: Alecto, the Fury. Throughout classical mythology, these female avengers are among the most vicious actors, wreaking havoc in their wake. Finally, near the end of the tale, Juno makes a dynamic show of power worthy of Mars himself, as she "[sweeps] down from heaven, [smites] with her own hands the bars and [flings] open the doors" of Janus's temple. Hamilton explicitly states that Juno uses "her own hands" to commit this violent action, emphasizing that the goddess has the power to act independently and forcefully on certain occasions. This causes the reader to question whether the goddesses must rely on other gods to achieve their goals, or whether they only do so because they find such tactics more expedient.

Dido, the primary human female in this tale, seems to be the ultimate passive female. As she becomes involved with Aeneas, she loses her independence and personal strength, her boundless love for him ultimately proving her downfall. Like so many other women in *Mythology*, Dido is wronged, abandoned, and humiliated by the man to whom she has pledged her devotion. But Dido is more than a pathetic figure: She is also a cautionary tale. For "The Adventures of Aeneas" suggests that a human woman can only maintain her authority and her sense of self if she remains free of romantic attachments. Camilla, the menacing warrior maiden, seems to owe her power to the fact that she "disdains" marriage, preferring "the chase and the battle and her freedom." The other formidable human female, the Sibyl of Cumae, lives alone in a cave and is completely free of relationships, male or otherwise. Even Dido, it must be remembered, was a wise and fearsome sovereign before she fell in love—through divine manipulation—with Aeneas, founding a city in a foreign land and leading it to greatness. Her love for Aeneas ruined her, and she seems to signal her rejection of that weakness when she coldly ignores the weeping Aeneas in the Fields of Mourning.

"The Adventures of Aeneas" explores various expressions of female power, from the manipulation of males to the rejection of the same. However, it is also important to note that one of the most important forces in classical mythology—the Fates—are represented as explicitly female figures to whom all individuals, man or woman, human or deity, are ultimately subject. The fact that three females could, with their spinning—the most domestic of household tasks—manipulate destinies as easily as thread suggests that the classical Greek and Roman cultures were more than simple patriarchies, and that women were considered far more than mere passive objects.

# Glossary of Literary Terms

**ANTAGONIST**
    The entity that acts to frustrate the goals of the *protagonist*. The antagonist is usually another *character* but may also be a non-human force.

**ANTIHERO / ANTIHEROINE**
    A *protagonist* who is not admirable or who challenges notions of what should be considered admirable.

**CHARACTER**
    A person, animal, or any other thing with a personality that appears in a *narrative*.

**CLIMAX**
    The moment of greatest intensity in a text or the major turning point in the *plot*.

**CONFLICT**
    The central struggle that moves the *plot* forward. The conflict can be the *protagonist*'s struggle against fate, nature, society, or another person.

**FIRST-PERSON POINT OF VIEW**
    A literary style in which the *narrator* tells the story from his or her own *point of view* and refers to himself or herself as "I." The narrator may be an active participant in the story or just an observer.

**HERO / HEROINE**
    The principal *character* in a literary work or *narrative*.

**IMAGERY**
    Language that brings to mind sense-impressions, representing things that can be seen, smelled, heard, tasted, or touched.

**MOTIF**
    A recurring idea, structure, contrast, or device that develops or informs the major *themes* of a work of literature.

**NARRATIVE**
    A story.

#### NARRATOR
The person (sometimes a *character*) who tells a story; the *voice* assumed by the writer. The narrator and the author of the work of literature are not the same person.

#### PLOT
The arrangement of the events in a story, including the sequence in which they are told, the relative emphasis they are given, and the causal connections between events.

#### POINT OF VIEW
The *perspective* that a *narrative* takes toward the events it describes.

#### PROTAGONIST
The main *character* around whom the story revolves.

#### SETTING
The location of a *narrative* in time and space. Setting creates mood or atmosphere.

#### SUBPLOT
A secondary *plot* that is of less importance to the overall story but may serve as a point of contrast or comparison to the main plot.

#### SYMBOL
An object, *character,* figure, or color that is used to represent an abstract idea or concept. Unlike an *emblem,* a symbol may have different meanings in different contexts.

#### SYNTAX
The way the words in a piece of writing are put together to form lines, phrases, or clauses; the basic structure of a piece of writing.

#### THEME
A fundamental and universal idea explored in a literary work.

#### TONE
The author's attitude toward the subject or *characters* of a story or poem or toward the reader.

#### VOICE
An author's individual way of using language to reflect his or her own personality and attitudes. An author communicates voice through *tone, diction,* and *syntax.*

# A Note on Plagiarism

Plagiarism—presenting someone else's work as your own—rears its ugly head in many forms. Many students know that copying text without citing it is unacceptable. But some don't realize that even if you're not quoting directly, but instead are paraphrasing or summarizing, *it is plagiarism* unless you cite the source.

Here are the most common forms of plagiarism:

- Using an author's phrases, sentences, or paragraphs without citing the source
- Paraphrasing an author's ideas without citing the source
- Passing off another student's work as your own

How do you steer clear of plagiarism? You should *always* acknowledge all words and ideas that aren't your own by using quotation marks around verbatim text or citations like footnotes and endnotes to note another writer's ideas. For more information on how to give credit when credit is due, ask your teacher for guidance or visit www.sparknotes.com.

# Review & Resources

## Quiz

1. What is given to Cronus to eat instead of his son, Zeus?

    A. A bull
    B. His twin brother
    C. A rock wrapped in baby's clothes
    D. His son, cooked by his wife

2. How does Prometheus anger the gods?

    A. Giving fire to humankind and tricking Zeus
    B. Seducing Zeus's wife Hera
    C. Demanding that men worship him as a god
    D. Rejecting Aphrodite's love

3. How does Odysseus escape Polyphemus's cave?

    A. A cap of invisibility and winged sandals
    B. Wine, a very sharp stick, and lots of rams
    C. A hollow wooden horse
    D. A winged horse and a magic spear

4. In what practice do the flower myths of Hyacinth and Adonis probably have their roots?

    A. Human sacrifice
    B. Homosexuality
    C. Adultery
    D. Cannibalism

5. How does Psyche betray Cupid?

    A. Cheating on him with another god
    B. Stealing his magic bow and arrows
    C. Telling her sisters who he is
    D. Seeing what he looked like

6. What famous couple does the story of Pyramus and Thisbe most closely resemble?

    A. Anthony and Cleopatra
    B. Pygmalion and Galatea
    C. Romeo and Juliet
    D. Napoleon and Josephine

7. Without whose help would Jason not have gotten the Golden Fleece?

    A. Hercules'
    B. Perseus's
    C. Medea's
    D. Teiresias's

8. How does Signy avenge her father's death?

    A. Poisoning her brother
    B. Enchanting the murderer in a ring of fire
    C. Destroying the Golden Fleece
    D. Locking her husband and their children in a burning house

9. What does Bellerophon foolishly try to do?

    A. Fly up to Olympus
    B. Duel with Apollo
    C. Usurp his father's throne
    D. Drive the Sun's chariot

10. What is the name of Daedalus's son?

    A. Theseus
    B. Minos
    C. Perseus
    D. Icarus

11. For what is Perseus most famous?

    A. Killing the Minotaur
    B. Killing Medusa
    C. Killing the Sphinx
    D. Killing the Hydra

12. How does Theseus cause his father's death?

    A. Poisoning his robe
    B. Accidentally hitting him with a discus
    C. Forgetting to change his ship's sail
    D. Angering King Minos

13. What does Theseus supposedly invent?

    A. Democracy
    B. The Labyrinth
    C. A way to raise the dead
    D. The constellations

14. Which of the following does Hercules *not* accomplish?

    A. Killing the Nemean lion
    B. Saving Theseus from Hades
    C. Killing the Calydonian boar
    D. Removing all the feces from the Augean Stables

15. From which three goddesses does Paris have to choose the fairest?

    A. Aphrodite, Athena, and Hera
    B. Demeter, Hera, and Persephone
    C. Aphrodite, Demeter, and Hestia
    D. Aphrodite, Artemis, and Athena

16. Which of the following were all great Greek heroes in the Trojan War?

    A. Achilles, Odysseus, and Aeneas
    B. Hector, Priam, and Cadmus
    C. Theseus, Hercules, and Perseus
    D. Menelaus, Agamemnon, and Ajax

17. Why is Achilles killed by an arrow in his heel?

    A. His heel armor had been stolen by Apollo.
    B. The arrow that killed him was dipped in Hector's poison.
    C. The gods, attempting to make Achilles invulnerable, had hidden his heart in his heel.
    D. His mother had been holding him by the heel when she dipped him in the River Styx.

18. Why did the Trojans take the gigantic wooden horse within the city's walls?

    A. If they did not, they would offend Aphrodite.
    B. The Greeks expected them to leave it outside the gates, which they implied would offend Athena.
    C. They were desperate for firewood after years of siege.
    D. Zeus himself had given it to them.

19. Whose heart does Aeneas break?

    A. Lavinia
    B. Psyche
    C. Medea
    D. Dido

20. About how long is Odysseus away from Ithaca?

    A. Two years
    B. Ten years
    C. Twenty years
    D. Fifty years

21. The myths served many functions for the Greeks. Which of the following purposes did they *not* serve?

    A. Literature, functioning as entertainment and pure fantasy
    B. Science, explaining the mechanics of the physical world
    C. Prophecy, showing how the world will end
    D. Religion, explaining the role of gods and morality in everyday life

22. What is Odysseus the only man ever to do and survive?

    A. Sailing past Scylla and Charybdis
    B. Descending to Hades and safely returning
    C. Hearing the song of the Sirens
    D. Attracting Circe's love

23. Of what city is Aeneas is considered the "real" founder?

    A. Rome
    B. Byzantium
    C. Athens
    D. Thebes

24. In Norse mythology, on what day is the world destined to end?

    A. Woden's day
    B. Yggdrasil
    C. Ragnarok
    D. Asgard

25. With whose help does Clytemnestra slaughter her husband, Agamemnon?

    A. Orestes
    B. Aegisthus
    C. Cassandra
    D. Electra

**ANSWER KEY**

1: C; 2: A; 3: B; 4: A; 5: D; 6: C; 7: C; 8: D; 9: A; 10: D; 11: B; 12: C;
13: A; 14: C; 15: A; 16: D; 17: D; 18: B; 19: D; 20: C; 21: C; 22: C;
23: A; 24: C; 25: B

## Suggestions for Further Reading

ARISTOTLE. *Poetics*. Trans. Gerald Else. Ann Arbor: University of Michigan Press, 1970.

BOWMAN, LAUREL. *Timeline of Greek History and Literature*. Victoria, Canada: University of Victoria, 1996.

BURN, A. R. *The Pelican History of Greece*. New York: Penguin Books, 1965.

BUXTON, RICHARD. *The Complete World of Greek Mythology*. London: Thames & Hudson, 2004.

HAMILTON, EDITH. *The Greek Way. New York:* W. W. Norton, reprint edition 1993.

HAMMOND, N. G. L., and H. H. SCULLARD, eds. *The Oxford Classical Dictionary,* 2nd ed. Oxford: Clarendon Press, 1970.

NIETZSCHE, FRIEDRICH. *The Birth of Tragedy and The Case of Wagner*. Trans. Walter Kaufmann. New York: Vintage Books, 1967.

RAWLINSON, GEORGE. *Ancient History*. New York: Barnes & Noble Books, 1993.